WHO SHOULD PAY FOR COLLECTING TAXES?

FINANCING THE IRS

C. Eugene Steuerle

American Enterprise Institute for Public Policy Research
Washington, D.C.

C. Eugene Steuerle directs finance and taxation projects at the American Enterprise Institute. He also has held positions with the Treasury Department, the Brookings Institution, and the American University.

Distributed by arrangement with

UPA, Inc.
4720 Boston Way
Lanham, MD 20706
3 Henrietta Street
London WC2E 8LU England

Library of Congress Cataloging in Publication Data

Steuerle, C. Eugene, 1946–
  Who should pay for collecting taxes?

  (AEI studies ; 448)
  1. United States.   Internal Revenue Service.   2. Tax administration and procedure—United States.   I. Title.
II. Series.
HJ5018.S84   1986   353.0072'4   86–22345
ISBN 0-8447-3610-4
ISBN 0-8447-3609-0 (pbk.)

AEI Studies 448

Printed in the United States of America

Contents

6   Summary and Conclusions   66

Recommendations   69

Appendix   71

List of Tables

List of Figures

Foreword

Because of major restructuring of the U.S. income tax, as well as large federal budget deficits, attention has been turned in recent years to the ways government activity is financed. Although revenues depend in part upon tax rates and tax bases, they also are affected by the way the tax laws are administered.

In this study Dr. Eugene Steuerle, director of finance and taxation projects at AEI and former economic staff coordinator for the landmark 1985 Treasury tax reform study, examines the administration of the tax laws. He pays special attention to the process that funds the Internal Revenue Service and to ways of improving that process.

Dr. Steuerle offers several important policy conclusions. He says that the IRS should receive modest increases in budget resources and that the benefits of increased enforcement currently outweigh costs and forestall raising the tax rates of honest taxpayers. Increases in resources devoted to enforcement will probably result in a revenue increase several times as much as the costs incurred. In many cases, however, the IRS is saddled with programs that are essentially unadministrable; additional resources for enforcement will not solve those policy problems. Moreover, many deficiencies in tax administration result less from a lack of resources or from the total size of staff than from government policies that restrict allocating revenues to hire qualified personnel in key areas.

Dr. Steuerle also concludes that the budget process for determining funding levels for the IRS is totally inadequate. Decisions are made within both the executive branch and the Congress without proper weighting or consideration of various benefits and costs. In the past, too much focus was put on the cost of higher levels of federal employment, while large federal deficits raise the specter of future overemphasis on the benefits of increased revenues from enforcement. In some cases, changes in policy have been accompanied by misleading statements about the effects of those changes on tax administration.

PAUL W. MCCRACKEN
President
American Enterprise Institute

Preface

This volume complements a growing series of working papers and analyses of tax and budget issues produced by AEI's Fiscal Policy Studies Program. The program recognizes that fiscal policy is determined not just by broad aggregates such as deficits and public expenditures, but also by the discrete budget and tax policies that give rise to those aggregates.

From one perspective, the Internal Revenue Service is the principal administrator of the fiscal policy of this country. So many revenue and expenditure-type policies flow through this agency that attention must be paid to the ways it administers these policies. Moreover, as demonstrated by Dr. Steuerle, deficits and tax collections themselves are affected by the extent to which the agency's activities affect compliance levels and revenues from enforcement.

Although this study focuses on a single government agency, it has implications for government-wide budget and personnel policies. Dr. Steuerle finds that some IRS deficiencies are caused by a budget process that gives inadequate weight to long-term benefits, accounts mainly in cash-flow terms, and denies the use of capital budgeting. Other difficulties arise in the hiring and retaining of personnel with skills such as computer programming. In many cases, one cannot solve these problems for the IRS without simultaneously addressing the effect of the broader budget and personnel policies on all agencies of government.

JOHN H. MAKIN
Director, Fiscal Policy Studies
American Enterprise Institute

Acknowledgments

This study was funded by grants from the Section of Taxation of the American Bar Association, the American Institute of Certified Public Accountants, and the George Gund Foundation. Countless persons have provided helpful advice and information, including Dave Attianese, Walt Bergman, Bill Cunningham, Larry Dildine, Terry Draver, Roscoe Egger, Albert Ellentuck, Marius Farioletti, Barbara Flickinger, William Forst, Kenneth Gideon, Rusty Guritz, Thomas Johnson, John Jones, Jr., Jerome Kurtz, Allen Lerman, John Makin, Harry Meyers, Clara Penniman, Wendell Primus, Kenneth Ryder, Jr., John Scholz, Frank Seidl, John Shannon, Kent Smith, Kenneth Thomas, David Weiner, Ann Witte, Dianne Woodbury, and, in IRS, Tom Andretta, Norman Bolz, Dennis Cox, Fred Cox, Bill Hildebrandt, Eli Intrator, Thomas Laycock, Bill Lefbom, Frank Malanga, Daniel O'Brien, Jr., Fritz Scheuren, Frank Sergovic, Fred Swick, Stephen Taylor, John Wedick, Chuck Wey, and Warren White. These individuals have not only been more than generous with their time, but also have shown a dedication to trying to understand the issues, to stating problems clearly, and to avoiding what is perceived by some as a potential crisis in the administration of the tax laws. All errors in this manuscript, of course, remain my own. Special thanks go to Martha Sheppard for her coordination and handling of the manuscript and to Rob Schilit for research assistance. Finally, I am deeply indebted to my wife, Norma, and my daughters, Kristin and Lynne, for the continuous support they offer me.

Although some suggestions and criticisms are offered in this manuscript, they should in no way be interpreted as comments upon the performance of any official. The IRS officials known to me all undertake their duties with the highest degree of integrity, competence, and desire for public service. The search for scapegoats in public life, especially among officials who are necessarily limited in time and resources, is unproductive and disabling. The denigration of public officials, in fact, is probably responsible for some of the problems of tax administration that are present today. In appreciation of the outstanding dedication of IRS personnel to the public, therefore, I dedicate this manuscript to them.

C. Eugene Steuerle
American Enterprise Institute

1
Introduction

The purpose of the IRS is to collect the proper amount of tax revenues at the least cost to the public, and in a manner that warrants the highest degree of public confidence in our integrity, efficiency and fairness. To achieve that purpose, we will: Encourage and achieve the highest degree of voluntary compliance in accordance with the tax law and regulations; Advise the public of their rights and responsibilities; Do all things needed for the proper administration and enforcement of the tax laws; Continually search for and implement new, more efficient and more effective ways of accomplishing our Mission.

IRS Mission Statement

Tax administration can never expect to be a popular function of government. When individuals and businesses pay taxes, they bear the costs of government activity. These costs include not only direct payments made to the government, but also those costs that derive from filing returns, keeping records, and being made subject to examination and audit.

Taxes, like most costs, are undesirable in and of themselves. They are justified only by the benefits and services they finance. The development of a safe defense, a social security system, and other components of modern government requires the simultaneous development of a fair and efficient system of tax administration. Tax administration in the United States is performed by the Internal Revenue Service (IRS), an agency envied in many parts of the world for its ability to limit noncompliance with a minimum of harassment to the ordinary taxpayer. The latest IRS mission statement, adopted in 1984, reveals a good deal about the agency: its concern with the integrity of staff and with its role in society; its recognition of multiple goals of revenue raising, compliance, and public dissemination of information; and its attention to the efficiency of its processes.

The agency's ability to perform its mission ultimately depends upon the sufficiency of its funding. This study is undertaken for several reasons. First, special concern has been raised in recent years about the adequacy of IRS operations. Second, the stringency of the federal budget, together with the need for revenues to finance rate reduction and other types of tax reform, has made tax administration an area of renewed attention by policy makers. Third, the IRS budget process seems haphazard at best, with dollars proposed for tax administration recently bouncing up and down like a ping pong ball.

To judge the adequacy of current funding levels and the suitability of current methods of financing the IRS, however, several related factors need to be examined. The history of past financing must be reviewed, and the ability of tax administrators to deal with alternative sources of noncompliance must be distinguished. One must also weigh both the benefits and costs that would be associated with any additional enforcement efforts. Alternatives to enforcement, including both policy changes and reallocations of existing resources, must be considered. Finally, the efficiency of the budget process can be improved only if the forces driving it are understood.

The level of financing for tax administration must represent the judgment of society, not of any one individual. This study argues that the benefits and costs of tax administration are inadequately considered under existing processes and that potential revenues from increased enforcement are likely to be well in excess of budgetary costs. Also proposed are methods of reducing noncompliance without an increase in enforcement. In the end, however, improved compliance is valuable primarily for the greater equity that it engenders in the distribution of tax burdens. The optimal funding level for tax administration therefore requires a careful balancing of the marginal costs of compliance against the perceived societal value of incremental equity improvements stemming from that compliance.

2
A Brief History of the IRS

The Internal Revenue Service was established by an act of the Congress on July 1, 1862. Before that time, the United States relied mainly upon customs duties and related taxes on shipping and imports and only infrequently upon internal taxation.[1] Since 1862, the IRS has grown steadily as the role of the federal government has expanded. The ratification of the Sixteenth Amendment to the Constitution in 1913 gave the IRS the function for which it is principally known today: the administration of corporate and individual income taxes.

Although the cost of administering the tax laws has increased over time, relative to collections it has held fairly steady, if not actually declined. Figure 2-1 shows the relationship between operating costs and collections for the IRS for the years 1900–1985.[2] This ratio has always been fairly low. Since World War II, costs have fluctuated between $38/100$ and $58/100$ of 1 percent of collections, standing at $48/100$ of 1 percent in 1985. A postwar comparison of U.S. civilian resident population to IRS personnel tells somewhat the same story. In 1947 there was one IRS employee for every 2,327 civilian residents, and in 1985 one for every 2,568.[3] IRS employment grew more slowly than population until 1960 (when the ratio reached 1 to 3,493); the trend has reversed since then.

In recent years, the IRS has also kept statistics on total staff years and dollars spent for various program units such as computer services, examinations, and returns processing. Staff years have increased from 66,900 in fiscal year 1972 to an estimated 93,700 in fiscal year 1986 (see table 2-1). Although budgetary cycles have caused both decreases and increases over this period, the general trend has been slightly upward.

Relative to various measures of workload, however, IRS resources have probably declined rather than increased. Figure 2–2, for instance, demonstrates the increase in total returns filed relative to IRS staff years. Other measures of workload also show significant increases. For example, congressional action in 1969 and in 1974 eventually led to the creation of units devoted to employee plans and to exempt organizations, both of which require over 2,250 staff years

3

TABLE 2–1
STAFF YEARS DEVOTED TO VARIOUS PROGRAM UNITS, FISCAL YEARS 1972, 1980, AND 1986

Program Unit	Staff Years			Increase in Staff Years			
				1972–1986		1980–1986	
	FY 1972	FY 1980	FY 1986	Number	Percentage	Number	Percentage
Automated data processing and information technology[a]	161	929	4762	4601	2858	3833	413
Information returns program	448	2941	4962	4514	1008	2021	69
Taxpayer service	2078	4977	4578	2500	120	-399	-8
Tax forms and publications	306	569	562	256	84	-7	-1
Appeals and tax litigation	2217	2719	3578	1361	61	859	32
Accounts receivable	7895	9402	12,201	4306	55	2799	30
Tax fraud investigations	3214	4395	4346	1132	35	-49	-1
Delinquent returns	2066	2287	2688	622	30	401	18
Examinations	24,075	28,104	28,431	4356	18	327	1
Employee plans	0	1404	1604	1604	—	200	14
Management services	0	0	1237	1237	—	1237	—
Exempt organizations	0	887	778	778	—	-109	-12
Research initiative	0	0	102	102	—	102	—
Returns processing	21,551	24,476	21,490	-61	0	-2986	-12
Internal audit	476	575	460	-16	-3	-115	-20
Enforcement litigation and technical rulings	1591	1564	1423	-168	-11	-141	-9
Executive direction	147	142	127	-20	-14	-15	-11
Statistics of income	667	610	395	-272	-41	-215	-35
Service Total	66,892	85,981	93,724	26,832	40	7743	9

NOTE: Data not final for 1986.
a. Numbers are not strictly comparable, as 1972 and 1980 estimates were for computer services only, while some ADP functions fell in other divisions. Similar limitations apply because of other reorganizations.
SOURCE: Internal Revenue Service.

FIGURE 2–1

OPERATING COSTS AS A PERCENTAGE OF COLLECTIONS, 1900–1985

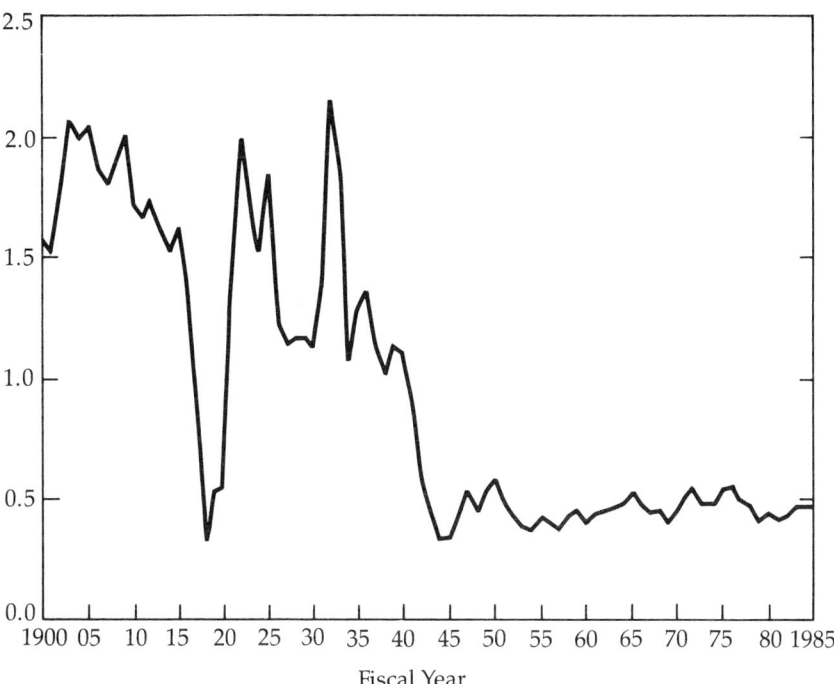

SOURCE: Annual Reports of the Commissioner of Internal Revenue, 1900–1985, Department of the Treasury, Internal Revenue Service.

to operate at present levels. Furthermore, taxpayers have been re-
questing more service, with telephone requests rising from 28 million
in fiscal year 1972 to an estimated 37 million in fiscal year 1986.[4]

Major Shifts in Responsibilities and Functions

The real story of the transition to the modern IRS is still hidden in
these figures. Overall, it is probably fair to say that the postwar era has
not seen a significant shift one way or the other in the level of
resources devoted to tax administration. On the other hand, there
have been important changes in responsibilities and functions within
the IRS. Most dramatic have been the increasing complexity of the tax
laws and the resource reallocations within the IRS in response to new
possibilities for improved administration and enforcement.

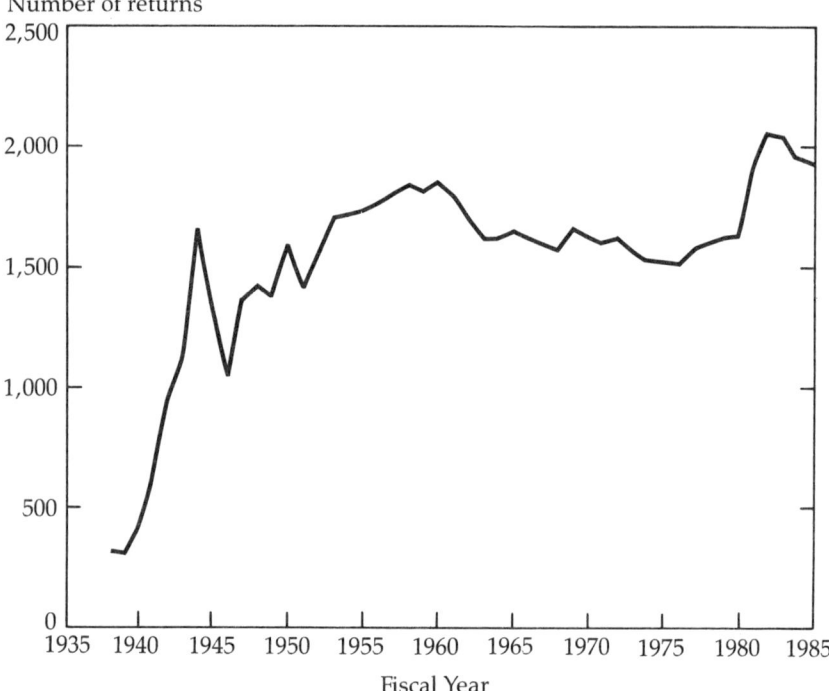

FIGURE 2–2
RETURNS FILED PER IRS STAFF YEAR, 1938-1985

Number of returns

Fiscal Year

SOURCE: Annual Reports of the Commissioner of Internal Revenue, 1938–1985, Department of the Treasury, Internal Revenue Service.

Complexity. The increased complexity of tax administration is reflected in several factors. First has been the tendency of policy makers to increase the number of deductions, credits, and exclusions in the tax code. As a related matter, the use and value of existing special preferences—and the organizational structures needed to take advantage of such preferences—have expanded significantly. In recent years, for instance, individuals have used partnerships as tax-sheltering vehicles. Partnerships have grown rapidly, not just through new investment but also through purchases of assets from corporations. Partnerships increased from 914,000 in 1965 to 1,514,000 in 1982, while the number of partners increased over the same period from 2,722,000 to 9,765,000.[5] Growth in the number of organizations adds to the number of returns that the IRS must handle, while increases in the use of deductions, exclusions, and credits in the code add to the number of items that must be tracked and sometimes examined or audited.

Second, there has been a substantial change in the frequency with which changes in the tax code occur. Enactments of major tax changes took place only once every several years in the 1950s and 1960s, but during the past decade there has been an important restructuring of the tax code almost every year. Many of these changes added to the complexity of the tax system and certainly to the difficulty faced by taxpayers in filling out their returns. The number of rules and regulations continues to expand accordingly.

Third, IRS officials claim that the amount of time necessary to examine returns has increased significantly because tax returns are much more complex.[6] This increased complexity stems from the expansion of deductions, credits, and exclusions mentioned above, to the related increase in the number of tax forms that must be filed, and also to the increased sophistication of tax practitioners—both the taxpayers themselves and professional preparers—in using various tax provisions to their maximum advantage.

Allocations of Resources among Functions. Like most organizations, the IRS has adapted over time to various needs and exigencies. It has shifted its resources to meet the demands placed upon it and has taken advantage of technological improvements to make its operations more efficient. The computer has especially affected the operations of the IRS and has allowed great enhancements in productivity. Returns are processed more quickly. Many errors of calculation by taxpayers are detected automatically. Despite their incompleteness, more and better statistics on taxpayers are recorded and analyzed. Methods of choosing which taxpayers to audit have been computerized, and resources are better allocated for raising revenue.

Along with the increased capabilities provided by the computer have come increased responsibilities. Requirements for information reporting to the IRS have expanded tremendously in the past few decades. In 1962, for example, Congress required payers of interest and dividends to file information reports with the IRS, and in 1984 reporting was expanded to cover such items as capital gains and interest on government securities. The IRS estimates that between fiscal 1976 and fiscal 1987 information returns will almost double from 472 million to 931 million, and staff years devoted to information returns programs will increase from approximately 1,700 to 5,767.

The increased workload, however, is reflected not merely in the number of documents that have to be processed. IRS personnel have millions of additional contacts with taxpayers. These contacts are

7

often computer-generated; the computer not only calculates the existence of the deficiency and often estimates the amount of tax owed, but also handles the correspondence until such time as human interaction becomes necessary.

Table 2–1 shows staff years devoted to various program units for 1972, 1980, and 1986, with the order of listing established by the percentage increase between 1972 and 1987. Many of the major increases are related directly or indirectly to improvements made possible by computer technology. The increase in staff years devoted to automated data processing and information technology is only the most direct example. The information returns program has expanded significantly and has become a major source of compliance revenues. Even the expansion of the delinquent returns program primarily reflects efforts to capture nonfilers through computer checks on taxpayers who report less than revealed through information returns or who discontinue the filing of returns in any one year. Increased downstream costs arise from development of these new capabilities as litigation increases, revenue agents are pulled in to examine returns found by computer to have underreported income and as persons working on accounts receivable keep track of and pursue taxpayers who are unable to pay their tax penalties and interest immediately. Thus, the number of personnel devoted to both tax litigation and accounts receivable has grown by over 30 percent since 1980.

The effect of these resource reallocations has been twofold. First, despite many current problems, the IRS as a whole has become more efficient in the collection of taxes. Computer manipulation of data is much easier than manual efforts, and economies have been achieved in the processing of returns and in almost all activities that require the recording of tax data. Many efforts, such as checks on individuals who had underreported only modest amounts of interest and dividends, also were not cost effective or economical in the past. Manual audits, for instance, would have cost more in resources than they would have collected in revenues. Now, computer audits of underreporting have become cost effective.

One result of this improvement in efficiency has been an increase in enforcement revenues. Figure 2–3 shows the IRS's estimate of enforcement revenues—defined as revenues from examination, delinquent returns, document matching, and accounts receivable—for fiscal years between 1980 and 1986. Although the accounts receivable figure may not really represent returns from enforcement, as some of these delayed bills would have been paid without additional administrative efforts, the increase is nonetheless substantial by almost any method of comparison.

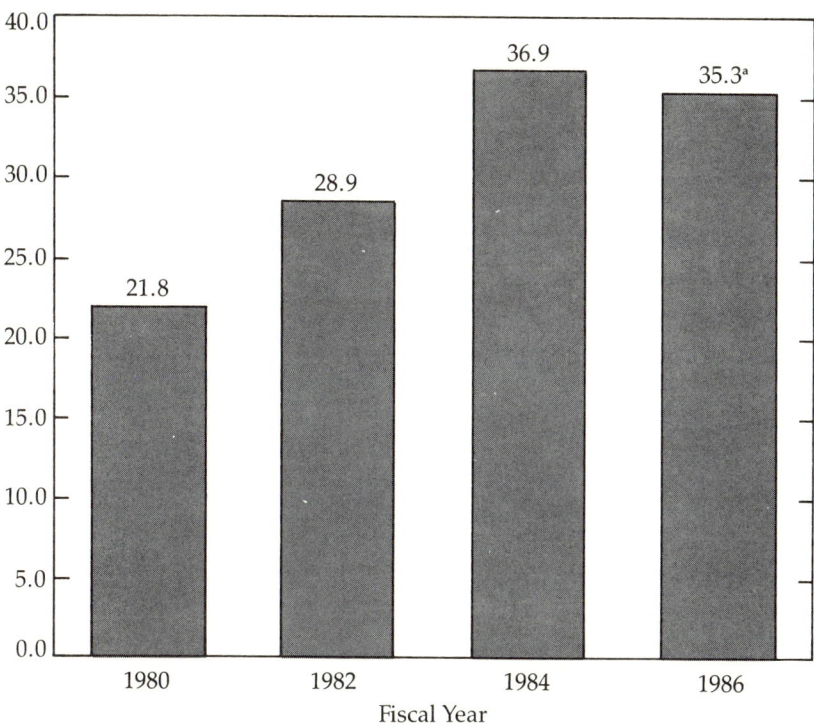

FIGURE 2–3
REVENUES FROM DIRECT ENFORCEMENT ACTIVITY, FISCAL YEARS 1980-1986
(billions of FY 1986 constant dollars)

Fiscal Year

a. For FY 1986, direct enforcement revenue collection is derived as follows: examination, $13.3 billion; delinquent returns, $5.0 billion; document matching, $3.0 billion; and accounts receivable, $14.0 billion.
SOURCE: Internal Revenue Service

The second effect of resource reallocation has been more noticed. To channel resources into new functions and areas where efficiency can be improved at least cost, other functions have been deemphasized and smaller, less politically sensitive functions began to lose resources. The Statistics of Income Division, which has responsibility for measuring who pays which taxes and for providing important information for national income measurement, was cut back severely. Despite the passage of major tax acts, regulations related to those acts were issued slowly because of limited staffing. Total tax fraud investigations have declined in recent years, and general tax fraud investiga-

9

tions (which exclude special investigations in areas such as drugs and narcotics) were conducted only about half as often in 1986 as in 1976 (3,475 versus 7,036).[7] Finally, more examination of receipts reported on information returns was accompanied in part by less examination of other receipts and deductions of taxpayers, an issue to which we turn next.

Examination and Audit of Tax Returns

Over the past quarter of a century, a declining percentage of returns have been subjected to direct examination by the IRS. Table 2–2 shows that examination coverage (examinations divided by filings) has fallen from around 5 percent in the mid-1960s to roughly 2½ percent in the mid-1970s and to less than 1½ percent by the mid-1980s. An increase in both the number and complexity of tax returns has contributed to this drop. Increased workload, however, is only part of the explanation. Over these years the IRS has also become much more efficient at directing resources toward those returns that have the highest probability of large, detectable errors. In addition, the examination division itself began special efforts that absorbed large proportions of available resources. A significant percentage of the best trained examination personnel, for example, has recently been devoted to tax shelters alone.[8]

This decline in the exam coverage rate can easily be cited as a potential compliance problem and has been used to justify recent congressional budget initiatives to increase IRS resources. The nature of the problem, however, must be put in perspective. As table 2–2 shows, the number of revenue agents and tax auditors has actually increased slightly since 1964, although there have been slight reductions between 1975 and 1985 during a period of significant growth in number of returns. The efficiency of the division itself improved, as changes in the amount of recommended tax and penalties demonstrate. Moreover, coverage statistics can be misleading. Auditing complex returns can take a great deal of time, and lower coverage rates inevitably result from further concentration of personnel on more complex returns. As one example, the IRS devotes over one-third of its technical staff to corporations (see table 2–3) even though reallocation of some of this staff to individual returns would result in much higher coverage rates.

It is even questionable whether IRS presence among taxpayers has declined. The examination division contacts taxpayers for reasons other than complete examination, and these contacts have held roughly steady over the past two decades. As a consequence, total

TABLE 2-2
EXAMINATION TRENDS, FISCAL YEARS 1964–1987

Fiscal Year	Revenue Agents & Tax Auditors (staff-years)	Filings (millions)	Examinations[a] (millions)	Percent Coverage	Contacts[b] (millions)	Percent Contacts[b]	Percent Presence[a]	Recommended Add'n Tax and Penalties ($ millions)	Recommended Add'n Tax and Penalties per Staff-Year ($ thousands)
1964	15,733	64.7	3.47	5.12	—	—	5.12	2.6	162
1965	15,576	67.6	3.33	4.92	—	—	4.92	2.7	175
1966	15,666	69.5	3.34	4.80	—	—	4.80	3.1	202
1967	15,999	72.2	3.01	4.16	—	—	4.16	3.3	207
1968	16,577	74.9	2.80	3.74	—	—	3.74	2.9	178
1969	15,636	76.7	2.43	3.17	—	—	3.17	3.9	252
1970	15,807	78.8	1.89	2.40	—	—	2.40	3.1	196
1971	15,909	81.3	1.54	1.89	—	—	1.89	3.4	214
1972	16,593	79.7	1.55	1.94	.43	.57	2.51	3.4	207
1973	16,523	79.6	1.65	2.08	.43	.54	2.62	5.1	309
1974	18,343	83.4	1.98	2.38	.63	.76	3.14	5.9	322
1975	19,027	86.4	2.20	2.56	1.22	1.41	3.97	5.3	277
1976	18,548	89.2	2.30	2.59	1.74	1.94	4.53	5.1	277
1977	18,137	88.0	2.15	2.44	.76	.87	3.31	5.1	279
1978	18,237	91.3	2.09	2.29	.49	.54	2.83	6.3	343
1979	18,305	93.0	2.08	2.24	.50	.54	2.77	7.2	393
1980	18,448	96.7	2.05	2.12	.53	.55	2.67	9.6	517
1981	17,214	99.3	1.83	1.84	1.03	1.04	2.88	10.7	624
1982	17,343	100.5	1.64	1.63	1.30	1.29	2.92	12.0	692
1983	17,354	102.0	1.59	1.56	1.35	1.32	2.88	14.1	813
1984	16,864	101.4	1.34	1.31	1.15	1.12	2.44	14.7	873
1985	17,067	103.4	1.38	1.34	.74	.79	2.13	17.7[c]	1,038
1986[d]	18,432	111.4	1.27	1.14	1.09	1.04	2.18	14.7	798

a. Does not include employment, excise, or windfall profit taxes.
b. From information returns program or other notice from examinations. Data not kept before 1972.
c. 1985 tax and penalties involved an unusually high reduction of inventories.
d. FY 1986 in the 1987 congressional submission.
SOURCE: Internal Revenue Service.

11

TABLE 2–3
TOTAL TECHNICAL STAFF DEVOTED TO EXAMINATION, 1985

Total	17,868
Individuals	9,752
Corporations	5,866
Estate	726
Partnership	687
Other	837
Addendum:	
Tax shelter program	2,235[a]

NOTE: Technical staff includes revenue agents, tax auditors, and tax examiners.
a. As compared to 14 in 1977, 342 in 1979, 1,286 in 1981, and 1,185 in 1983.
SOURCE: Internal Revenue Service.

exam presence—examinations plus contacts—has not declined as dramatically as outright exam coverage. Moreover, the increased devotion of other resources in the IRS to information returns, delinquent filers, and other programs has made the agency's presence felt in other ways. Although no series of historical statistics on the total presence of the IRS were available, the millions of computer-generated letters now sent to taxpayers indicate that the presence of all divisions has almost certainly increased rather than decreased over time.

IRS officials nonetheless express considerable worry over the decline in examination coverage. Are such worries justified? In table 2–4, the estimated presence and exam coverage of taxpayers for 1985 is broken down by various classes of taxpayers. An overall exam coverage rate of 1.34 percent in 1985 allowed 86.77 percent coverage of corporations with $100 million or more in assets, but only 0.69 percent coverage of corporations with under $50,000 in assets and 2.02 percent coverage of individuals with $25,000 to $50,000 of income.[9] Also shown in the table are estimated compliance figures derived from comprehensive audits that are conducted in conjunction with the Taxpayer Compliance Measurement Program (TCMP). Although audits are incapable of detecting all noncompliance, the figures clearly demonstrate substantial noncompliance in a great many taxpayer classes for which audit coverage remains quite low.

From another perspective, the IRS has become more and more efficient at enforcing that portion of the tax system where withholding and information reporting are operative. For taxpayers with income only from wages, interest, and dividends, with few or no deductions or credits, and without income from independent contracts or busi-

TABLE 2–4
EXTENT OF EXAMINATION BY CLASS OF TAXPAYER, FISCAL YEAR 1985

Class of Taxpayer	Percent Presence	Percent with Exam Coverage	No. of Examiners	Percent Estimated Compliance
Individuals				
Less than $10,000				
1040A	.93	.35	257	84.3
Non 1040A	1.02	.44	221	72.1
$10,000-$25,000				
Simple	1.22	.64	489	95.1
Complex	2.25	1.67	874	88.5
$25,000-$50,000	2.60	2.02	2,448	94.7
$50,000 and over	4.11	3.53	2,506	92.8
Business				
Non-farm				
Under $25,000	2.03	1.45	346	66.3
$25,000-$100,000	3.13	2.55	780	76.0
$100,000 and over	5.98	5.40	1,381	74.8
Farm				
Under $25,000	2.11	1.53	60	70.4
$25,000-$100,000	2.36	1.78	133	76.4
$100,000 and over	4.94	4.36	257	77.8
Total Noncorporate Income	1.89	1.31	9,752	—
Corporations				
No Balance Sheet	—	1.56	92	63.0
Under $50,000	—	.69	176	46.2
$50,000-$100,000	—	1.49	162	62.4
$100,000-$250,000	—	1.42	212	67.3
$250,000-$500,000	—	1.73	150	78.6
$500,000-$1 Mil	—	2.55	164	81.5
$1 Mil-$5 Mil	—	5.76	433	88.0
$5 Mil-$10 Mil	—	15.04	193	90.7
$10 Mil-$50 Mil	—	25.19	486	—
$50 Mil-$100 Mil	—	48.27	281	—
$100 Mil and over	—	86.77	3,517	—
Total Corporations	—	2.40	5,866	—
Total Income	—	1.34	15,618	—
Other[a]	• n.a.	n.a.	2,250	—
Total Program	—	1.12	17,868	—

— = not available.
n.a. = not applicable.
a. Includes estate and partnership audits.
SOURCE: Internal Revenue Service.

ness, the IRS has a variety of devices short of examination by which to detect underpayment of taxes. For perhaps the majority of taxpayers, therefore, the system is more efficient than ever at collecting taxes. What has fallen by the wayside are IRS attempts to examine those items of income, expense, or deductions for which there is no readily available source of information other than the taxpayer.

A legitimate fear, therefore, is not that direct pick-up of penalties and interest is inadequate, but that levels of examination coverage may be so low in some cases that noncompliance is encouraged. As taxpayers realize that their probability of being audited is low, many will be encouraged to underreport income and overreport expenses for which only an audit can result in a detection of error.

Some Recent Problems

It is difficult, of course, to determine whether a decline in certain IRS efforts stems from a reallocation of resources to other efforts or from a failure to fund all areas adequately. In fact, the issues are not separable, as both total funding and its allocation ultimately determine IRS effectiveness. Moreover, the policies that must be enforced are determined outside the agency by Congress and by the president. These policy choices are the primary determinants of IRS functions, allocations, and resource needs.

Some recent problems within the IRS highlight the ways in which difficult resource questions in one part of the agency can have effects elsewhere:

• The IRS updated its computers under a Service Center Replacement System (SCRS) improvement program and replaced much of its equipment in 1983 and 1984. As soon as the system was near completion, the service center's computers were discovered to be inadequate for the job. "Contributing factors include the fact that SCRS was originally planned as a strict *rollover* of existing processing operations, so it was sized to allow for only 8% annual growth. No allowance was made for self-initiated enhancements or additions common to a system of this size and complexity. In addition, [the vendor] sized the system very tightly, leaving no margin for error or capacity for enhancements."[10]

• In the 1985 filing season, the IRS experienced severe processing delays in sending out refunds and handling other items for taxpayers. In trying to replace its computer system (that is, in implementing the SCRS program mentioned above), the IRS discovered too late that there were problems in the hardware, the software, and the operation of the new system.[11]

- In the third quarter of 1984, 26,000 business taxpayers made timely quarterly payments of tax at their depository banks. The Philadelphia Service Center, however, continually made bad tapes or improperly labeled its tapes, so that these payments could not be credited to the right businesses. These taxpayers received numerous letters claiming underpayment of tax. Although these notices were eventually halted, final correction of the error was not made until some taxpayers had received several notices, including final notices.[12]
- Tax shelters remove a large percentage of resources from other enforcement functions. In fiscal year 1979, tax shelter exams accounted for only 1.7 percent of revenue agent workload, but by fiscal 1984 this number had grown to 19.1 percent.[13] About 24 percent of pending tax court cases at one point in 1985 involved tax shelters.
- Between fiscal year 1982 and fiscal year 1986, accounts receivable rose from $20.5 billion to over $43.5 billion.[14]
- In 1985 inventory levels for returns processing were at extraordinarily high levels. Yet the administration forced a cutback of personnel in the returns-processing area substantially in excess of that recommended by the IRS. In 1986, however, substantial hiring of returns-processing personnel took place. In fact, spending in much of 1986 was taking place at an annual rate well in excess of that technically allowed by many of the continuing resolutions under which the IRS was operating. Yet until the summer no one either in the executive branch or in Congress was able to take the responsibility for reducing personnel (and risking another filing season failure) or for increasing the budget (and violating various independent budget goals).
- In 1976, 1978, and 1980, the IRS did not have a budget before the fiscal year started. Since 1980, the IRS has had no budget either before or during the year, but instead has been functioning on a series of continuing resolutions.[15]

Other problems have recently come to light, including the destruction of correspondence in the Austin service center.[16] Most of these problems involved some amount of human error and were to some extent avoidable. One has the feeling, however, that the IRS in recent years has been in a no-win situation. Although it has succeeded in pulling a cloth over one bare spot after another, each movement of the cloth has only uncovered new bare spots. The IRS can reallocate personnel to different areas, but the cost of eliminating one problem is often only the creation of another. These current problems, many of which have been reported in the popular press, focus renewed attention on the difficulties of tax administration. In the following chapters this study demonstrates alternative ways of avoiding these types of problems in the future: (1) adding resources to the IRS, after weighing appropriate benefits and costs at the margin; (2) reducing the number of programs or policies that the IRS is asked to enforce; (3) allowing tax administrators greater flexibility in resource allocation—in particular, to hire needed personnel in certain key areas; and (4) improving the budget process itself.

Sources of Noncompliance

Much recent research has been directed at estimating the level of noncompliance with the tax system or, in more popular terms, the size of the underground economy.[17] This study does not review that literature. Nonetheless, determining the amount of resources to be devoted to the IRS requires some understanding of both the levels and the types of noncompliance in the United States. In recent years, the IRS has attempted to measure the size of the tax gap. Table 2–5 breaks down these estimates for various years by broad categories of income and deductions.

Although the tax gap is estimated to have grown recently, much of that growth has coincided with an increase in the federal government's general revenues. We are not that concerned with the question of whether average compliance has or has not improved: the figures are still large enough to be of concern. In our view, moreover, existing statistics have enough sources of error to make any purported answer highly debatable. In a long-term sense, there have probably been two offsetting trends. First, there is a belief expressed by some officials that fewer moral qualms are attached to cheating. On the other hand, the increasing sophistication of businesses and organizations has meant that more payments have fallen into systems where the accounting is good, where cheating is more detectable, and where the IRS is more likely to be supported by withholding and reporting systems.

Several aspects of noncompliance are highlighted in the table. First, underreported income (income is defined here essentially as receipts before deductions) is a much more serious compliance problem than overstated deductions. The reasons are twofold: receipts are well in excess of deductions (there would likely be no tax base otherwise); and IRS examiners express the view that deductions, exemptions, and expenses are much easier to audit because a lead—the taking of the deduction—is already reported by the taxpayer. In the case of many receipts, existence of the item itself must be proven.

Second, much of the gross tax gap is concentrated in those areas for which there are no withholding or reporting systems. This can be gleaned in part from table 2–5 and partly from table 2–6, which breaks down certain sources of income by voluntary reporting percentages. Compliance is best where withholding (wages) or reporting (interest and dividends) has been well established.

Third, excluding informal suppliers, about two-fifths of the total compliance gap is estimated to come from noncorporate businesses, rental real estate, farms, and partnerships. Before one jumps to the conclusion that there are different degrees of honesty between the self-employed and other groups, again note that these are the areas in which almost no withholding and reporting system exists. Because only an audit can detect error in the income and deductions of the self-employed, a few underreport large amounts of income, for instance, by reporting no income at all.

It is also important to note that the combined effect of income and deductions makes the underreporting of net income larger for the self-employed. For most other taxpayers, deductions are only a small percentage of receipts. Indeed, a typical taxpayer will take no itemized deductions and have income from wages and interest only. For businesses, however, expenses are large relative to receipts, and errors can compound. Table 2–7 uses a slightly different data source— estimates of underreporting that can be detected by examiners through the Taxpayer Compliance Measurement Program—and shows how a 5.3 percent understatement of total income (receipts) and a 7.5 percent overstatement of deductions can result in a 32.0 percent understatement of net income for businesses of the self-employed.

TABLE 2-5
ESTIMATES OF TAX GAP, 1973–1981
($ billions and percent)

Category	1973	1976	1979	1981
Gross Tax Gap[a]	28.7 (100.0%)	39.0 (100.0%)	61.8 (100.0%)	81.0 (100.0%)
Income underreported on filed returns	17.3 (60.3%)	24.2 (62.1%)	38.4 (62.1%)	52.2 (64.4%)
Business, rents, royalties[b]	6.2 (21.6%)	8.7 (22.3%)	13.8 (22.3%)	18.8 (23.2%)
Dividends and interest	2.4 (8.4%)	3.4 (8.7%)	5.4 (8.7%)	7.3 (9.0%)
Capital gains	2.4 (8.4%)	3.3 (7.7%)	5.2 (8.4%)	7.1 (8.8%)
Wages and salaries[c]	2.1 (7.3%)	2.9 (7.4%)	4.6 (7.4%)	6.3 (7.8%)
Partnerships and small business corporations	1.7 (5.9%)	2.4 (6.2%)	3.8 (6.1%)	5.2 (6.4%)
Informal suppliers	1.5 (5.2%)	2.1 (5.4%)	3.4 (5.5%)	4.6 (5.7%)
Other[d]	0.6 (2.1%)	0.9 (2.3%)	1.3 (2.1%)	1.7 (2.1%)

Pensions and annuities	0.4 (1.4%)	0.5 (1.3%)	0.9 (1.5%)	1.2 (1.5%)
Items overstated and tax underreported	5.5 (19.2%)	6.4 (16.4%)	9.7 (15.7%)	12.9 (15.9%)
Overstated personal deductions[e]	3.4 (11.8%)	3.0 (7.7%)	5.0 (8.1%)	6.6 (8.1%)
Overstated business expenses[f]	2.1 (7.3%)	3.4 (8.7%)	4.7 (7.6%)	6.3 (7.8%)
Remittance gap[g]	1.5 (5.2%)	2.4 (6.2%)	5.3 (8.6%)	6.8 (8.4%)
Nonfilers[h]	0.9 (3.1%)	1.4 (3.6%)	2.0 (3.2%)	2.9 (3.6%)
Corporate tax	3.5 (12.2%)	4.6 (11.8%)	6.4 (10.4%)	6.2 (7.7%)

a. Excludes tax gap from drugs, prostitution, and other parts of the illegal sector, estimated at $9.0 billion for 1981.
b. Nonfarm proprietor income (except informal supplier income), farm proprietor income, rents, and royalties.
c. Tip income estimated at 40.7 percent of wage and salary reporting gap for 1981.
d. Estates and trusts, state income tax refunds, alimony, miscellaneous.
e. Includes itemized deductions, personal exemptions, and statutory adjustments.
f. Expenses overstated from: Schedule C, business; Schedule F, farm; Schedule E, rental; plus estimated overstatement for partnerships, estates and trusts, and small business corporations.
g. Individual balance due after remittance estimated at 64.7 percent of remittance gap for 1981; employer underdeposit of withholding was the other major component of remittance gap.
h. Net of prepayments and credits.
SOURCE: "Income Tax Compliance Research: Estimates for 1973-81," Department of the Treasury, Internal Revenue Service, July 1983.

TABLE 2-6
Voluntary Reporting Percentages for Individual Filers and Nonfilers, by Source of Income,[a] 1973–1981

	1973	1976	1979	1981
Wages and salaries[b]	95.4	94.9	94.4	93.9
Dividends	90.7	87.1	85.7	83.7
Interest	87.6	88.1	86.3	86.3
Capital gains	75.7	64.3	63.4	59.4
Nonfarm proprietor income and partnership and small business corporation income[c]	84.0	82.2	80.7	78.7
Farm proprietor income	88.6	92.6	89.5	88.3
Informal supplier income	20.7	20.7	20.7	20.7
Pensions and annuities[b]	81.5	85.3	85.0	85.2
Rents	94.7	94.0	95.4	95.6
Royalties	74.3	65.6	64.2	61.2
Estate and trust income	82.0	79.2	75.7	76.2
State income tax refunds, alimony, and other income	66.0	55.2	62.3	62.0
Total income	91.2	90.4	89.8	89.3
Wages and salaries	95.3	94.9	94.4	93.9
Pensions and annuities	83.5	86.9	86.7	86.9

a. Gross income only. When overstated expenses are also taken into account, reporting percentages fall significantly for certain items such as proprietor and rental income.
b. Before correcting for pensions misreported as wages. After this correction the voluntary reporting percentages would be modified as shown below:

c. Does not include informal supplier income.
SOURCE: "Income Tax Compliance Research: Estimates for 1973-1981," Department of the Treasury, Internal Revenue Service, July 1983.

TABLE 2–7
SUMMARY OF SOURCES OF UNDERREPORTING OF NET PROFIT
FOR SELF-EMPLOYED BUSINESSMEN, 1982

Categories	(1) Amount Reported ($ billions)	(2) Amount That Should Have Been Reported ($ billions)	(3) Net Understatement or Overstatement[a] (percent)
Total income	214.1	226.2	5.3
Total deductions	163.9	152.5	7.5
Net profit or loss[b]	50.1	73.7	32.0

a. Col. (3) = |Col. (2) − Col. (1)|/Col. (2)
b. Details may not add because of rounding.
SOURCE: Taxpayer Compliance Measurement Program for 1982. Amount underreported reflects only those amounts detectable by audit.

Notes

1. Internal Revenue Service, *Internal Revenue Service Manual* (Washington, D.C.: U.S. Department of the Treasury), 1985, pp. 1100-3–1100-4.

2. Internal Revenue Service, *Annual Report of the Commissioner,* various reports, 1900-1985 (Washington, D.C.: U.S. Department of Commerce). Methods of accounting for expenses and personnel have changed significantly over this period.

3. Internal Revenue Service, *Annual Report of the Commissioner,* 1947 and 1985 (Washington, D.C.: U.S. Department of Commerce, 1947 and 1985).

4. Data on IRS resources and workload were provided by the Internal Revenue Service.

5. Statement of Ronald A. Pearlman, Assistant Secretary of the Treasury for Tax Policy, before the U.S. House of Representatives, Subcommittee on Oversight of the Committee on Ways and Means, September 20, 1985.

6. See chapter 3 for measures of average staff time devoted to examining tax returns.

7. See footnote 4.

8. Table 2–3 shows the growth in examination technical staff devoted to tax shelters up to 1985.

9. For these purposes, the income measure used by the IRS is total positive income—that is, income before allowing the subtraction of negative declarations of such items as partnership income. These latter items often include tax shelters.

10. Internal Revenue Service, Statement of the Assistant Commissioner for Computer Services, October 29, 1984.

11. Statement of Johnny C. Finch, senior associate director, General Government Division, U.S. General Accounting Office, before the U.S. House of

Representatives, Subcommittee on Oversight of the Committee on Ways and Means, March 4, 1986.

12. General Accounting Office, *Fact Sheet to Congressional Requestors, Tax Administration: Information on IRS' Philadelphia Service Center,* November 1985, and *Briefing Report to Congressional Requestors, Tax Administration: How IRS' Philadelphia Service Center is Addressing Processing Problems,* March 1985.

13. Donald E. Wilt, "Trends in DIF and DIF-Related Service Examinations," in *1986 Update: Trend Analysis and Related Statistics,* Internal Revenue Service, pp. 47–56.

14. Statement of Johnny C. Finch, General Accounting Office, before the U.S. House of Representatives, Subcommittee on Oversight, Committee on Ways and Means, May 12, 1986.

15. See statements and discussions by Hugh Calkins and Albert B. Ellentuck before the Subcommittee on Oversight, Committee on Ways and Means, U.S. House of Representatives, on Staffing levels and Allocations of Resources of the Internal Revenue Service, May 12, 1986. Washington, D.C., Superintendent of Documents, forthcoming.

16. See Attachment II to the Statement of Johnny C. Finch, General Accounting Office, before the Subcommittee on Oversight, Committee on Ways and Means, U.S. House of Representatives, on IRS Service Center Operations, December 16, 1985.

17. Among the many articles on the size of the underground economy are the following: American Institute of Certified Public Accountants, *Underreported Taxable Income: The Problem and Possible Solutions* (Washington, D.C.: Federal Taxation Division, 1983); E. L. Feige, "How Big Is the Regular Economy?," *Challenge* 22 (November-December 1980), pp. 5–13; Peter M. Gutmann, "The Subterranean Economy," *Financial Analysis Journal* 33 (November/December 1977), pp. 26–28; ICF Inc., *Summary of Public Attitude Survey Findings,* prepared for the Research Division, Internal Revenue Service, U.S. Department of the Treasury, 1985; K. A. Kinsey, "Survey Data on Tax Compliance: A Compendium and Review," American Bar Foundation Tax Compliance Working Paper 84-1, American Bar Association, December 1984; and Vito Tanzi, *The Underground Economy in the United States and Abroad* (Lexington, Mass.: D.C. Heath and Company, 1982). For an especially useful summary, see James S. Henry, "Noncompliance with U.S. Tax Law—Evidence on Size, Growth and Composition," in Phillip Sawicki, ed., *Income Tax Compliance: A Report of the ABA Section of Taxation Invitational Conference on Income Tax Compliance* (American Bar Association, 1983, pp. 15–111).

3
Yields and Costs
of Additional IRS Efforts

There are obviously limits to how far the IRS or any administrative agency can go in reallocating resources to meet additional demands. Indeed, we have seen how past reallocations by the IRS at times have caused new problems elsewhere within the organization. The question of whether more resources should be made available to the agency therefore cannot be avoided. This chapter assesses some of the benefits and costs to society of adding resources for tax enforcement and administration.

The benefits of additional enforcement accrue mainly to compliant taxpayers. If the costs of additional enforcement are greater than the revenues raised—that is, if yields are less than costs—then tax rates on all taxpayers would actually need to increase to maintain the same level of government services in the economy. If, on the other hand, yields exceed costs, then the net increase in revenues can be used to reduce tax rates and tax burdens for compliant taxpayers. It is this type of calculation that often focuses attention on whether or not the yield-to-cost ratio exceeds unity.

The previous chapter shows that revenues from enforcement historically have tended to be well in excess of costs. History also demonstrates that many increases in enforcement revenues stem from the implementation of fairly discrete and cost-effective projects, two prominent examples being the information returns program and the delinquent filers program. It is highly likely that the IRS would devote future increases in financing to new programs that promise comparable effects on revenues to be raised. In 1986, for example, high marginal yields were estimated for improved automated matching of information returns with tax returns. While extrapolation of this type of historical experience may be warranted, each new idea still must be judged on its own merit.

An alternative and more conservative approach is to project the expansion of existing programs rather than the development of new ones. Any major expansion of the existing enforcement activity of the IRS would almost inevitably be concentrated on the examination function, an area that consumes about one-third of IRS resources and the majority of its enforcement budget. If a reasonable estimate of marginal yield from examination can be made, then it would provide a minimum bound on the enforcement yield possible from an increase in overall IRS resources.

Marginal Yields and Costs of Examinations

For fiscal year 1985, the *average* yield to cost is estimated as 10.7 for examination (and 13.9 for all enforcement programs).[1] In estimating the amount of revenues available from increased resources, however, marginal—not average—yields must be determined. Because returns and activities with the greatest potential are often pursued first, marginal yields for expanding existing activity will generally be less than the average yields. Maximum revenue for a given amount of expenditures theoretically will be secured when the marginal yield-to-cost ratios for small expansions of all activities are the same. Such a theoretical solution, however, is complicated by the discrete nature of many projects that are not divisible into small, marginal components. In addition, the IRS pursues many goals, and their success cannot be measured by enforcement revenues achieved per dollar of expenditure. Finally, for a given amount of expenditures on enforcement, *maximum revenue is achieved when maximum compliance, not maximum enforcement revenue, is attained.* Thus, one method the IRS uses to encourage compliance is to ensure that some minimum level of audit coverage applies to every income class even when enforcement yields are thereby reduced.

Within the examination division, marginal estimates are generated by the Examination Resources Allocation Model, or more informally, the Exam Model. Although marginal yields are also estimated for other activities both within and outside the examination division, any estimate of an increase in enforcement revenue associated with a large expansion of existing activity is dominated by the results that come forth from the Exam Model.[2] This model is therefore worth some attention if we are to assess the effects of changing the IRS budget.

The Exam Model and Discriminant Function Technique.[3] As a first step in the development and updating of the Exam Model, thorough TCMP audits are conducted for a sample of the taxpayer population. Checksheets are provided to examiners who record, line by line,

24

information on about two hundred items for each taxpayer audited. This information, including the amount of an item that was reported and the estimated amount that should have been reported, is transcribed onto computer files. Statistical analysis then determines those return characteristics that would best identify returns with potentially large tax errors and mathematically derives the weights, or relative importance, of different characteristics.

The statistical technique used by the IRS and its contractors is known as discriminant function (DIF) analysis. For each examination class, two populations are separated: those with significant tax change and those with little or no tax change. Each income or deduction item is broken down into intervals—for example, charitable contributions between $1,000 and $2,000—and then tests are conducted to see which line items and which intervals are associated with tax returns having a large tax change. A DIF formula is developed to include significant items and intervals, and optimal weights are attached to these items. For each tax return, a DIF score can then be calculated by applying the derived weights to the related line items. Various DIF formulas are actually calculated for each class of taxpayer, as it is unclear at first which variables and interval lengths will work best. Alternative formulas are then compared according to criteria of productivity, average tax change, marginal tax change, and probability of no change. The best DIF formula for each class is then selected.

For projecting the results of normal (non-TCMP) audits, the Exam Model starts with the derived DIF formulas and then makes several adjustments. Any sample or population of returns can be ordered by their DIF scores or expected yield if audited. The IRS takes the ordering of returns generated by the TCMP sample and then fits a curve (based upon a particular mathematical functional form) through them much as one would fit a curve through any set of points on a graph. Such a curve may look like the top curve shown in figure 3–1. TCMP audits, however, are more comprehensive than regular audits. Based on historical experience, therefore, total projected yield from TCMP audits (say, for the top 2 percent of DIF scores) is then compared to the yield from regular audits (at the same coverage level). The formula for yields according to audit coverage is then scaled back by the relative difference in the two amounts, and a second yield curve for normal audits can then be calculated (see the lower curve in figure 3–1).

Experience from actual audits is also used to make cost calculations based upon time spent and the type of personnel used. The IRS currently uses an average cost figure to compare with marginal yields. Ideally, one would want to use marginal cost, but it is not known

FIGURE 3–1
HYPOTHETICAL YIELD CURVE FROM AUDIT

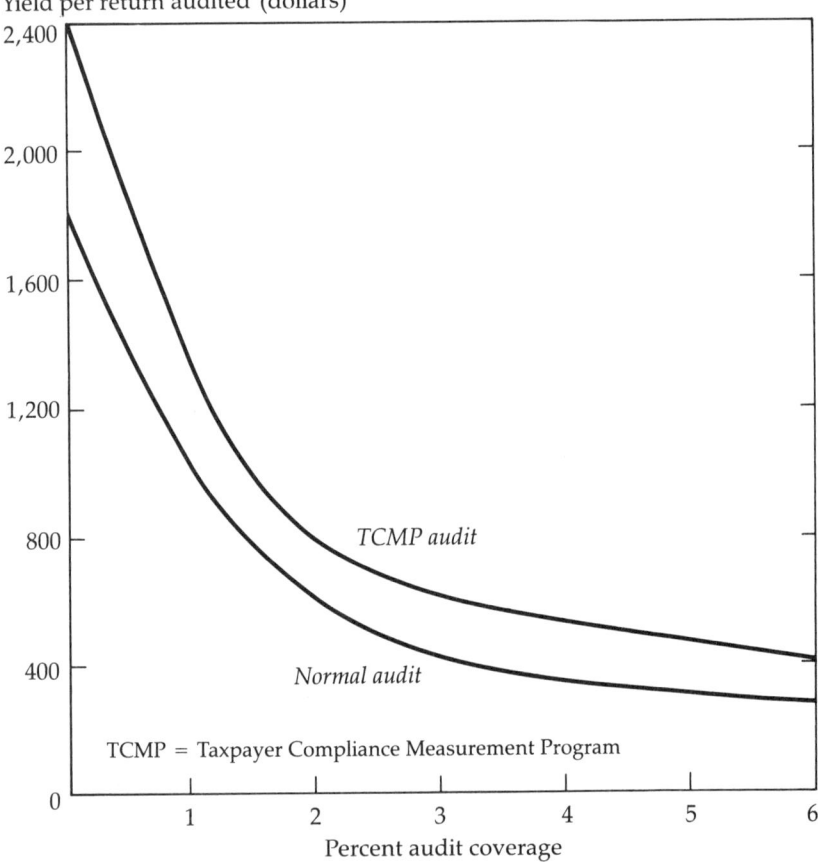

Yield per return audited (dollars)

TCMP = Taxpayer Compliance Measurement Program

Percent audit coverage

whether expansion of coverage would show greater marginal cost because of increased time spent in detecting errors, or lower marginal cost because of fewer line items to be examined. As with most statistical techniques, improvements can be made, and some suggestions are contained in the Appendix to this study. With one exception, it is unclear whether these suggested improvements would increase or decrease existing yield-to-cost estimates. The exception is the recommendation that the IRS cost figure include all governmental costs, not only those most relevant to the IRS budget. The major omission in moving from IRS costs to total governmental costs is that the value of pension rights accrued by employees is ignored. Since the budget of the U.S. government accounts poorly for these costs, it is not surprising that they are not counted well by the individual agencies. For making correct personnel decisions, Congress and the Office of Management and Budget (OMB) should nonetheless include these costs.

My overall assessment is that the methods used by the IRS are sound, well developed and technically competent. The IRS often turns to outside consultants and researchers to derive alternative DIF formulas and to improve its estimating techniques. Moreover, IRS procedures have been reviewed by others who have arrived at similar conclusions.[4]

For 1985, estimates of average yields, marginal yields, and average costs for most taxpayer classes are shown in table 3–1. The largest costs and the highest average yields are associated with the most complex returns and with individuals or businesses with the most income or asscts. For instance, we see that corporations yield almost two-thirds of additional tax, penalties, and interest even though only about one-third of technical personnel were devoted to corporate examination.

The decline in the yield curve is also revealed in this table. Marginal yields are less than average yields in all cases, and in some instances are significantly less. In cases where marginal and average yields are close to one another, the decline in the marginal yield/cost curve is more gradual. For instance, complex returns in the $10,000-$25,000 income range have average yields of $824, marginal yields of $633, and a marginal yield to cost of 3.0. Since only about 2 percent of these 10 million returns have exam coverage, one would suspect that yields would remain above costs even with a substantial expansion of coverage.

The table does give us a good idea of the marginal returns available from expansion of resources beyond fiscal year 1985 levels. If audit resources are directed first to individuals with $50,000 or more in income and to corporations with more than $50 million in assets, then fairly high marginal returns of over seven to one are available. After additional examination resources are devoted to these returns, the marginal yield-to-cost ratios will decrease, but ratios of more than four to one remain for a wide variety of other classes: individuals with less than $10,000, simple returns with income between $10,000 and $25,000, nonfarm businesses with $100,000 or more in assets, and so forth.

In summary, expansion of examination resources beyond 1985 levels should achieve marginal yields which are four to seven times as large as costs. This represents a minimum bound on enforcement

TABLE 3–1
YIELDS AND COSTS OF EXAMINATION, FISCAL YEAR 1985

Class of Taxpayer	Average Yield (dollars)	Marginal Yield (dollars)	Average Cost (dollars)	Marginal Yield Cost	Total Additional Tax, Penalties, Interest ($ millions)	Filings (thousands)
Individuals						
Less than $10,000						
1040A	1,579	780	148	5.3	132	20,806
Non 1040A	1,322	1,087	225	4.8	68	9,980
$10,000–$25,000						
Simple	842	615	155	4.0	133	20,622
Complex	824	633	226	3.0	165	10,025
$25,000–$50,000	1,069	678	235	2.9	582	22,410
$50,000 and over	6,727	3,624	501	7.2	2,048	6,874
Business						
Non-Farm						
Under $25,000	1,881	1,818	575	3.2	62	1,873
$25,000–$100,000	3,620	2,274	723	3.2	217	1,909
100,000 and over	10,334	5,187	1,224	4.2	691	1,004
Farm						
Under $25,000	2,371	2,044	627	3.3	13	286
$25,000–$100,000	1,429	1,226	746	1.6	14	467
$100,000 and over	8,828	5,598	1,242	4.5	115	241
Total Noncorporate Income					4,240	96,497

		Corporations				
No balance sheet	20,259	8,430	1,708	4.9	79	181
Under $50,000	3,871	2,578	1,443	1.8	30	813
$50,000–$100,000	4,540	3,549	1,448	2.5	30	343
$100,000–$250,000	6,904	5,425	1,573	3.5	55	444
$250,000–$500,000	6,472	455	1,622	3.4	37	261
$500,000–$1 Million	9,041	7,345	1,903	3.9	52	177
$1 Million–$5 Million	14,487	12,383	2,534	4.9	179	169
$5 Million–$10 Million	22,190	18,876	3,214	5.9	102	24
$10 Million–$50 Million	29,246	7,300	4,459	1.6	274	28
$50 Million–$100 Million	4,416	38,498	5,428	7.1	259	7
$100 Million and over	—[b]	—[b]	35,083	—[b]	10,215	8
Total Corporations					11,312	2,455
Total Income					15,552	98,952
Other[a]					1,457	31,054
Total Program					17,009[c]	130,006

a. Includes estate and partnership audits.
b. Coverage rate is too high to make calculation meaningful.
c. Excludes $628 million for additional service center contacts.
SOURCE: Internal Revenue Service.

revenues available, as expansion of other activities or the development of new programs may be even more productive.

Further Estimates of Yields from Expanded Resources

While the above data demonstrate what expansions of examination resources can achieve at the margin, we would also like to know what more sizable expansions may entail. Therefore, two additional methods of estimating potential enforcement revenues were adopted. The first method was to apply a restrictive set of assumptions to the Exam Model and to compare yields at two alternative levels of resources, both of which are substantially higher than 1985 levels; the second method was to apply regression techniques to historical data.

Examination Model Comparisons. The IRS is often asked to project yields at different levels of funding. Because of the way the requests are made, however, each projection uses a different baseline—a different year, a different starting level of resources, and so forth. For instance, an increase in resources for taxpayer service one year, if not funded by an increase in total funding, may result in a decreased budget for the examination division. For projecting marginal yields, the Exam Model would then start with a lower baseline, which in turn would imply a higher measure of yield to cost (since yield to cost declines as examination resources increase). Moreover, for budget purposes, the examination division often makes other changes in the model, such as increasing the resources allocated to the tax shelter program.

To control for these factors, two additional runs of the Exam Model were made in a manner that held constant these extraneous factors. The model was initially run under the assumption that technical personnel would number 22,185 in fiscal year 1988, a level of resources that eventually would be obtained under a revenue initiative proposed in 1986 that would increase total examination personnel by about 7,500 over the long run. From that baseline, technical personnel were again increased to 27,812. This increase of 5,647 technical personnel again represents an increase of about 7,500 total personnel, technical and nontechnical, or about double the increase discussed in the 1986 revenue initiative. Held constant in both runs were the examination rate of corporations with $100 million or more in assets and the amount of resources devoted to special projects such as tax shelters. The audit rate of these large corporations is too high to assume indefinite expansion, and projections of additional yields are highly questionable at that level of audit. Special projects such as tax shelters have characteristics that are sensitive to timing and design; they are really not part of the basic model, but are add-ons.

If these additional 7,500 staff were added to the increase already projected under the revenue initiative, and if the model allocated the staff only on the basis of obtaining maximum revenue, there would be an estimated increase in total costs of $328 million and in total additional tax, penalties, and interest of $872 million. The estimated yield-to-cost ratio for this increase is therefore about 2.7 to 1, slightly less than the marginal yield-to-cost ratios for many classes of taxpayers shown in table 3–1. In the latter case, of course, one was operating on an earlier part of the yield-to-cost curve—that is, before the addition of substantial numbers of personnel over and above fiscal year 1985 levels. Keep in mind once again that this type of ratio represents a minimum bound on possible returns, as many special projects both within and outside the examination division will often prove far more productive.

With 15,000 additional personnel, the examination division would increase in size by over 60 percent above 1985 levels. Even after such a sizable growth, marginal yields to costs *for even further increases* would fall in the 2.3 to 3.1 range for almost all types of returns. The yield-to-cost curve also tends to flatten out. For individuals, for example, the marginal yield to cost would still be 3.1 to 1 even after the staff increase of 15,000, while the ratio was 3.5 to 1 after an increase of 7,500. (The model showed lower yields for almost all corporate examinations, a result a bit different from the pattern shown in table 3–1.)

Regression Results. A second method of estimating changes in examination yield with changes in IRS resources was based on regression techniques. The dependent variable, recommended additional tax and penalties, is shown in the second-to-last column of table 3–1. This number is close to the IRS's estimate of additional tax, penalties, and interest actually collected, but differs slightly because of the inability to collect penalties assessed on some taxpayers, the payment of interest to the IRS, and certain other factors. In 1985, for instance, the IRS estimates that $17.7 billion was recommended and $17.0 billion was collected. Ideally, historical data would be available on actual collections and on enforcement revenues from other sources as well.

These recommended additional tax and penalties were then regressed on the following factors: total IRS costs, time, total IRS revenues, total number of returns, and a constant term. Only the first two variables were significant in the various regressions, and total IRS costs were always the most significant variable in any regression in which they appeared.

Two regression results are reported below:

Recommended tax and penalties = 3.9 x IRS costs;   (1)

Recommended tax and penalties = 8.1 x IRS costs,   (2)
less $589 million x time,

where 1964, the first year of the sample, is treated as year 1, 1965 as year 2, and so forth.[5]

The first equation indicates that recommended tax and penalties have generally run about four times the level of total IRS costs. The second equation implies that increasing IRS funding has been associated with an eight fold increase in recommended tax and penalties, but that this increase was partially offset by a negative time trend that is more difficult to explain. The latter term may indicate that when IRS funding is held constant in an economy with rising receipts and more complex returns, additional demands elsewhere in the system drain off resources, and enforcement revenues decline. For instance, tax-payer service could be expanded at the cost of a decline in enforcement efforts.

The insignificance of other variables implies that IRS costs are not simply a substitute for other factors such as total revenues. That is, increased enforcement revenue does not seem to be a function mainly of higher levels of tax reported on returns. Instead, increased enforcement revenue seems to be associated with increased resources, even after holding other factors constant.

While these regressions lend support to the hypothesis that additional IRS resources would lead to additional compliance revenues, the data themselves are limited. Many other untested factors could influence the level of compliance revenues. The relationship between costs and revenue increase probably changes over time with alterations in IRS capabilities; tax law changes and other economic events have an unknown effect on the results. It is statistically impossible to include so many factors in a regression of this type, for there are more plausible explanatory variables than there are observations.

Total Revenue Effect

The results from any method of estimating changes in enforcement revenues with changes in the levels of IRS resources should be treated with caution. Nonetheless, a review of previous IRS experience, extrapolation of the Exam Model, and regression results all support the notion that additions to IRS resources would lead to an increase in enforcement revenues several times larger than costs.

The goal of enforcement activities, however, is not an increase in direct enforcement yield, but rather an improvement in overall compliance. Data on overall compliance, however, have not been gathered for enough years to make any type of rigorous statistical analysis feasible. In addition, there are multitudes of factors—mores of society, complexity of tax laws, existence of withholding and reporting systems—that influence total compliance. It would be quite difficult, even with complete data on overall compliance, to determine the ultimate effect of additional enforcement activity.

The theoretical literature offers some limited help here. One basic conclusion is that, if individuals are risk averse, they are likely to cheat less as the probability of paying a penalty increases.[6] Even here, there is some debate as to the final effect of more audits on compliance.[7] For instance, if more audits reveal to taxpayers the inability of the IRS to capture certain types of information, then taxpayers could underreport even more of their income. On the other hand, audits may improve taxpayer knowledge and serve as a channel of information, especially when taxpayers err because of the complexity of the law.[8]

In the end, neither the empirical nor the theoretical evidence is adequate to provide certainty of result, and a judgment must be made. My own conclusion is that examination coverage levels are so low in many areas that taxpayers are beginning to realize how easy it is to underreport certain types of income and overreport certain types of deductions. Some taxpayers face almost zero probability of audit under the existing system. For them, existing enforcement practices are likely to have almost no deterrent effect with respect to those line items for which the more automatic withholding and reporting systems are inoperative. Accordingly, expansion of existing IRS enforcement efforts is likely to increase revenues by a multiple of the increase in direct yield from audit.

Social Yields and Costs

The benefits of better compliance with the tax laws are often misunderstood. There is no direct increase in productivity or total income in the economy as a whole associated with better compliance by individuals and businesses who currently do not report all income. Improved compliance is mainly a redistributive activity that creates a more equitable distribution of the tax burden between compliant and noncompliant taxpayers.

Some economic literature proceeds on the assumption that equity has no value in and of itself, and that the benefits of increased compliance are confined to such items as greater certainty of actual tax payments for risk-averse individuals (that is, for a given revenue yield, there is less variance of payments between audited and unaudited taxpayers).[9] While this literature is useful, it provides policy makers only limited help in addressing the question of whether or not IRS resources should be increased.

Perhaps the fundamental difficulty is the assumption that improved equity has no value in and of itself. Since all income is treated as being of equal value, the implicit assumption is that it is better for the tax burden of a compliant taxpayer to be $10 and that of a noncompliant taxpayer to be $5 than for the tax burden of each to be $8, with an additional dollar of real resources spent to induce compliance. Yet part of what people believe they are purchasing with their tax dollars is a set of governmental programs in which they are treated fairly. Many are willing to pay something additional to ensure the fairness of the system, regardless of any other benefits they may receive. For instance, the "efficiency" of the tax system could also be increased simply by imposing extraordinarily harsh penalties for noncompliance. These penalties may entail no additional real resource costs and therefore are more efficient than increased audit coverage. Nonetheless, such harsh penalties would so violate principles of equity that taxpayers indicate they are willing to "pay" the additional costs associated with more expensive ways of inducing compliance.

Improved compliance does have efficiency implications. Noncompliant activities and individuals are given a competitive advantage in the economy, leading to an inefficient allocation of resources. In addition, government in a democratic society is dependent upon the good will and trust of the people. Taxes support those activities of the government that are chosen by the people through their representatives. A tax system perceived as unfair can hamper the government's ability to perform well those beneficial functions for which it exists.

The costs of increased enforcement, however, are not trivial. The time and talent of enforcement personnel are diverted from the production of other goods in the economy, so that improved equity clearly comes at a price. The socially optimal level of enforcement, therefore, cannot be determined solely by whether marginal revenues to the government exceed the government's own costs.[10]

Other social costs exist as well. Audited taxpayers spend more time dealing with governmental personnel and less time engaging in activity that they value more or in producing goods and services for others. Some may view enforcement activities as harassment; even for compliant taxpayers, there are likely to be psychological costs such as worry and anxiety. When activity by any enforcement officials—police, administrators or regulators—rises, there is an increase in the intrusiveness of the government and a decrease in the privacy of citizens. No attempt is made here to put a price tag on items such as privacy and peace of mind, but they should be considered no less important than the direct costs of tax administration.

Notes

1. See Frank M. Malanga, "The Relationship Between IRS Enforcement and Tax Yield," Internal Revenue Service memo, 1986.

2. For enforcement planning and budgeting, the IRS is developing an Enforcement Resource Allocation Model. Planning models currently exist for examination, the information returns program (IRP), delinquent returns, and delinquent accounts. There are difficulties, however, with using models other than the Exam Model for assessing marginal yield/cost ratios at different resource levels. For IRP and delinquent returns, there are definitive programs that are often, although not always, fully funded. A high marginal yield may result from the slight expansion of some existing program, but only limited expansion is possible. What is more likely is that large amounts of additional revenues would be spent on the implementation of some new program or approach. For instance, IRP may expand to try to capture and use the newly available information on capital gains, or it may seek more optical scanning equipment to record more information returns. These choices are discrete, and the marginal returns involved have to be judged on a case-by-case basis. In the case of delinquent accounts, estimates of marginal returns are available, but they do not yet subtract out (present value) estimates of the revenues that eventually would be paid without the additional enforcement effort. Thus, some of the yield is merely accelerated payment.

3. This description is necessarily quite brief. The interested reader is referred to the following sources, among others: U.S. General Accounting Office, *How the Internal Revenue Service Selects Individual Income Tax Returns for Audit*, Report to the Joint Committee on Taxation, U.S. Congress, November 5, 1976; Internal Revenue Service, "The Examination Function," *Tax Administration Review*, December 1985, pp. 31–39; Internal Revenue Service, U.S. Department of the Treasury, "The Examination Resources Allocation Model," September 1985; Office of the Assistant Commissioner for Planning and Research, Internal Revenue Service, "Discriminant Function (DIF) Handbook," Document 6588 (Revised), November 1979.

4. Some review of the Exam Model is contained in the following documents: General Accounting Office, *How the Internal Revenue Service Selects Individual Income Tax Returns for Audit*, November 1976; Price Waterhouse, "IRS Resource Model: Analysis of Work Processing," October 1984; Karla L. Hoffman, Lambert S. Joel, and Martin H. Pearl, Center for Applied Mathematics, National Engineering Laboratory, National Bureau of Standards, Washington, D.C. "Resource Requirements and Allocations in IRS Audit

Division," Technical Report to the Audit Division, Internal Revenue Service, February 1979. The Grace Commission also reviewed the development of the Exam Model and based its recommendation for an increase in IRS examination personnel partly upon that review. See *The President's Private Sector Survey on Cost Control: A Report to the President* (Grace Commission Report), January 1984, p. 82.

5. For the first equation, the t-statistic = 15.9 and R-squared = .767. The t-statistics for the independent variables in the second equation equal 4.2 and -2.2, respectively, and R-squared = .811.

6. Some surveys have confirmed empirically this positive correlation between compliance levels and the probability of incurring payment penalties. Song and Yarborough, for example, constructed an index of tax ethics on the basis of a 1975 survey of taxpayers in eastern North Carolina, and concluded that the most important factor governing tax compliance was the fear of detection. They also found that tax ethics was worst among those who believed that tax evasion by others was common and among those who felt alienated, powerless, and distrustful. Westat, Inc. (1979) found that taxpayer uncertainty about the possibility of audits, collections, penalties, and investigation encourages compliance, and that successful noncompliance by some taxpayers encourages noncompliance by others. See Young-dahl Song and Tinslet E. Yarborough, "Tax Ethics and Taxpayer Attitudes: A Survey," *Public Administration Review*, September/October 1978, pp. 442–52; Westat, Inc., "Individual Income Tax Compliance Factors Study Qualitative Research Results," prepared for the Internal Revenue Service, 1979.

7. For an excellent survey on the factors affecting compliance, the reader is referred to: Ann D. Witte and Diane F. Woodbury, "What We Know about the Factors Affecting Compliance with the Tax Laws," *Income Tax Compliance: A Report of the ABA Section of the Taxation Invitational Conference on Income Tax Compliance*, Reston, Va., March 1983, pp. 133–48. Other relevant sources include the following: Thomas S. McCaleb, "Tax Evasion and the Differential Taxation of Labor and Capital Income," *Public Finance* 31, no. 2 (1976), pp. 287–94; Agnar Sandmo, "Income Tax Evasion, Labor Supply, and Nonlinear Tax Schedules," *Journal of Public Economics* 16, December 1981, pp. 265–88.

8. See John T. Scholz, "Coping with Complexity: A Bounded Rationality Perspective on Taxpayer Compliance," Proceedings of the Seventy-eighth Annual Conference of the National Tax Association-Tax Institute of America (NTA, 1985), pp. 30–38.

9. Relevant studies here include: Joel Slemrod and Shlomo Yitzhaki, "The Optimal Size of a Tax Collection Agency," Working Paper No. 1759, National Bureau of Economic Research, Cambridge, Mass., October 1985; Michael G. Allingham and Agnar Sandmo, "Income Tax Evasion: A Theoretical Analysis," *Journal of Public Economics*, November 1972, pp. 323–38; Shlomo Yitzhaki, "A Note on 'Income Tax Evasion: A Theoretical Analysis'," *Journal of Public Economics*, May 1974, pp. 201–02.

10. Among those who have discussed the relationship between revenue yield, the social cost of compliance, and compliance goals of the IRS are the following: Richard Goode, "Some Economic Aspects of Tax Administration,"

IMF Staff Papers, vol. 28 (1981), pp. 249–74; Roy Blough, *The Federal Tax Process* (New York: Prentice-Hall, 1952); Harold M. Groves, "Income Tax Administration," *National Tax Journal* 13, pp. 37–53; Carl S. Shoup, *Public Finance* (Chicago, Ill.: Aldine Publishing Company, 1969); and Diane F. Woodbury, "The Production Structure of Tax Administration: The Case of the Internal Revenue Service" (University of North Carolina, unpublished).

4

Alternatives to Enforcement

Increasing the amount of revenues available to the IRS is only one way to improve compliance. Three categories of alternative methods are discussed here: (1) policy changes to make the tax code more administrable; (2) a grant of greater authority to the commissioner and other IRS administrators to allocate revenue to hire necessary personnel; and (3) other approaches, including changes in penalties and in the ways the IRS affects taxpayer expectations.

The Effect of Policy on Administration

An administrative agency's functions are determined primarily by the laws it is assigned to enforce. When enforcement costs are large, the policies themselves must be called into question. A given policy may be meritorious from every standpoint except that it is difficult or expensive to administer; in that case, it may still be poor policy.

Over the years, governmental policies continually have been added to the Internal Revenue Code. Many are designed for worthwhile purposes: to promote investment, to encourage saving, to expand the availability of health care, to finance elections, to provide an incentive for the support of children and the elderly, and so forth. The implementation of all these policies has been assigned to the IRS, almost always with little consideration of their administrative implications and with no additional funding provided to cover costs.

Although the IRS is often criticized for its failures, Congress compliments the agency indirectly each time another tax deduction or credit is enacted. In effect, putting so much social policy into the tax code often reflects an implicit belief that the IRS has extraordinary administrative capability, or at least more capability than direct expenditure agencies that could be assigned to perform the same functions.[1]

With a few exceptions, the IRS is not organized along policy lines and does not have separate divisions or groups to deal with each "program." The functional organization of the IRS instead reflects the way in which the agency conducts its activity: examination, returns processing, taxpayer service, and so forth. Each additional credit or deduction is treated as one more item that must be recorded, audited, clarified through rules and regulations, and discussed with taxpayers who call for information. If the IRS were structured more like a business, it would be more likely to organize around the policies being implemented, and great care would be taken to measure the merits of each policy according to criteria such as expense, benefits provided, and ease of administration.

The IRS is not in charge of policy, only administration. Policy decisions are left to Congress and to the Office of Tax Policy within the Office of the Secretary of the Treasury. Because of these separations, the IRS is often unable to make policy judgments or to consider adequately the relationship between policy and administration.

The large budget cuts of the Statistics of Income Division is only one reflection of this myopic attitude toward the administrative effects of policy (see table 2–1). Although tax returns provide data on tax policies, the IRS will often fail even to measure the size or effect of particular policies through statistical sampling techniques. Statistical information takes a long time to gather and generally has only a limited effect on short-run enforcement and administration. Thus, when pressure is increased to expand taxpayer service, to send refund checks on time, or to increase enforcement revenues, a policy function such as the gathering of statistics will often be cut back to finance expansion or prevent contraction elsewhere. Recently, for instance, the IRS abandoned statistical analysis of the pension area even though early work had shown that existing estimates of wealth in pension plans could be in error by several hundred billion dollars. When a comprehensive review of pension policy is undertaken, as is likely in the next few years, much necessary information will not have been assembled.

Those in charge of policy, on the other hand, sometimes give only token heed to administrative considerations. At times policy makers are so involved in negotiating among themselves and with various interest groups that they have little political incentive to choose the policies that are most administrable. Indeed, once strategies have evolved, certain administrative problems may be kept under wraps and not revealed. In the major tax reform effort of 1974–1976, for example, each compromise along the way made greater use of a minimum tax and of passive loss limitations, even though policy makers were well aware that more direct approaches would have created far less administrative burden.

The budget process within both the executive branch and the

Congress is not designed to encourage examination of programs in the Internal Revenue Code. Broadly defined, the list of tax programs that affect the budget includes any credit, exclusion, deduction, exemption, or way of measuring income that leads to a tax that is different from the one that would apply to economic income under given statutory tax schedules. For administrative purposes, the list would also include those items of income or expense having special enforcement difficulties, such as tip income or charitable donations of artwork. The special analysis of tax expenditures in the budget of the U.S. government details many of these programs, although it generally fails to list items that are overtaxed due to multiple taxation. Even here, time constraints have prevented the executive branch from updating that list to include items identified in the recent Report to the President on Tax Reform for Fairness, Simplicity and Economic Growth.[2] Imagine again some private business spending millions or billions of dollars and not accounting for the total amount of the expense!

Even when accounting is done, no part of the budget process of either the executive branch or the Congress requires review of the working of the credit, exclusion, or deduction, or determination of how much should be spent on that item in the future. Unlike direct expenditure programs, there is no appropriation for most tax preferences. Consideration of any given program is done almost at random, with Congress or the executive branch often taking an interest in one tax program or another only after some new or spectacular revelation is made.

For IRS purposes, this means that the administrability of many policies will go unexamined for years or even decades. For some policies, however, changes in the law provide meaningful alternatives to greater enforcement.

Some Difficult-to-Administer Programs

While the IRS is not organized to do a program-by-program analysis, it does manage to keep line-by-line accounts of many items under its Taxpayer Compliance Measurement Program (TCMP). As noted before, the TCMP measures the amount of underreporting and overreporting that can be detected through comprehensive audit. These measures are the best available and therefore will be used here to give some idea of the problems prevalent in many tax programs.

Information on line items reported on individual income tax returns is provided in tables 4–1 and 4–2. Table 4–1 deals with overstated deductions, exemptions, and credits; table 4–2 covers understated income, receipts, and tax due. In both cases the line items are ordered according to the amount of overstatement or understatement as a percentage of the amount which should have been reported. The purpose of these tables is to determine which programs run by the IRS seem to be most administrable, as measured by rates of compliance attained. The ordering therefore reflects no judgment as to the merits of the policy goals of the programs.

In a large number of programs, the amount of overstatement is well in excess of 10 percent of the amount that should be reported. One wonders whether such a rate of error would be considered tolerable for a direct expenditure program. Take as an example the first line item in table 4–1, the exemption for dependents other than children and parents. It is estimated that relative to the dollar amount of such exemptions that should have been allowed, taxpayers claimed an additional 74.5 percent. Among other nonbusiness programs, large overstatements are present in earned income tax credits (44.9 percent), child and dependent care credits (27.1 percent), and moving expenses (19.5 percent). For items of business income, the worst error rates are for bad debts, jobs credits, travel and entertainment, and car and truck expenses, all of which have error rates between 18.3 percent and 43.1 percent and are overstated on 36.4 percent to 60.4 percent of returns.

A number of problems are also evident on the income or receipt side of the ledger. Table 4–2 displays net error rates for income items such as rental and royalty income. Since the amount of net income reported may be small or negative in some cases, the error rates will appear especially large because of the compounding effect previously demonstrated in table 2–7[3].

Understatement is particularly troublesome in the cases of tip income, tax on withdrawals from Individual Retirement Accounts (IRAs), and gains on business assets. Investment credits are difficult to recapture, with 26.9 percent of returns understating 21.9 percent of the amount that should have been reported. The alternative minimum tax that was present in 1983 resulted in an understatement of tax on 32.6 percent of returns. Partially taxable pension income showed a much higher error rate than fully taxable pension income (7.4 percent versus 1.8 percent). Wages, interest, and dividends—items on which there was either withholding or full reporting—had error rates between 0.2 percent and 4.2 percent.

Several caveats should be kept in mind in interpreting these tables. The error rates shown here are the best available, but they are not designed to answer important policy questions. They do not measure the full extent of underreporting, but only that detectable by

TABLE 4–1

OVERSTATED DEDUCTIONS, EXEMPTIONS, AND CREDITS, 1982

Category	Overstatement as a Percentage of Total[a]	Percentage of Returns with Overstatement[b]
Exemption for dependents other than children and parents	74.5	63.8
Exemption for parents	67.5	65.9
Total casualty or theft loss	58.7	73.5
Political contributions credit	53.6	49.2
Exemption for children living away from home	50.1	49.9
Earned income credit	44.9	51.5
Bad debts (business)	43.1	60.4
Employee business expenses	34.7	52.0
Jobs credit	33.0	52.0
Miscellaneous itemized deductions (other than casualty)	29.4	37.0
Child and dependent care credit	27.7	40.9
Travel and entertainment (business)	27.1	39.4
Moving expenses	19.5	48.5
Medical expenses	19.5	43.8
Car and truck expenses (business)	18.3	36.4
Investment credit	15.5	20.9
Insurance expenses (business)[c]	14.1	39.1
Noncash charitable contributions	14.1	20.8
Employee benefit programs	13.2	33.4
Exemption for children living at home	13.0	14.1

Elderly credit	12.9	18.1
Charitable contributions in cash	12.6	33.3
Residential energy credit	12.1	19.9
Alimony paid	11.9	38.8
Depreciation (business)	11.6	31.1
Pension and profit sharing plans (business)	10.6	14.2
Depreciation/depletion in rental/royalty property	10.0	26.8
Interest other than home mortgage	9.1	26.1
Taxes other than income and property	9.0	27.3
Exclusion for reinvested public utility dividends	8.3	7.2
Home mortgage interest paid to individuals	8.1	17.1
Real estate taxes	5.3	16.0
Payments to Keogh retirement plan	3.6	10.8
Dividend exclusion	3.4	4.8
Home mortgage interest paid to financial institutions	3.3	10.4
State and local income taxes	3.2	10.5
Payments to IRA	1.8	4.4
Wages paid by business	1.4	12.5
Deduction for working married couple	1.2	4.0
Exemption for taxpayer 65 or older	0.3	0.3
Wages and salaries	0.1	0.1
Taxpayer exemption	0.0	0.0

a. Amount of overstatement on returns with overstatement as a percentage of total that should have been reported.
b. Number of returns overstating the deduction, exemption, or credit as a percentage of number of returns that should have reported the item.
c. Many items of business expense are not displayed here. Items listed up to this point—bad debts, travel and entertainment, car and truck expense and insurance—were those having the worst TCMP compliance rates for business expenses.

SOURCE: Internal Revenue Service, Taxpayer Compliance Measurement Program for 1982 Returns, table 10.

TABLE 4-2

UNDERSTATED INCOME, RECEIPTS AND TAX DUE, 1982

Category	Understatement as a Percentage of Total[a]	Percentage of Returns with Understatement[b]
Total rental or royalty income	151.1	54.2
Advanced earned income credit payments	88.0	78.9
Uncollected employee social security tax on tips	76.2	81.9
Tax on an IRA	60.9	66.3
Gains on business assets (form 4797)	58.3	30.6
Tip income	40.2	52.7
Interest income from bearer obligations	40.0	65.5
Net profit from business	33.6	71.4
Recapture of investment credit	21.9	26.9
Self-employment tax	21.4	60.4
Capital gains distributions (not on Schedule D)	18.0	31.6
Interest income in seller-financed mortgages	16.1	28.5
Alimony received	14.9	16.6
Short-term capital gains (before losses)	13.3	19.0
Net farm rental profit	12.0	45.0
Unemployment compensation (taxable)	11.9	21.4
Long-term gains from small business corporations	11.1	5.9
Windfall profits tax	10.4	9.1

	a	b
State and local income tax refunds	10.1	15.4
Capital gains	9.6	22.1
Rental and royalty receipts	8.9	38.1
Partially taxable pensions and annuities	7.4	16.3
Long-term capital gains (before losses)	7.2	18.4
Alternative minimum tax	6.4	32.6
Ending inventory	6.3	9.9
Total business income (before deductions)	6.0	35.6
Gross dividends	4.2	22.4
Interest income	3.5	40.7
Farm income	3.0	31.3
Fully taxable pension, IRA, annuities	1.8	5.9
Wages, salaries, tips, etc.	0.2	3.9

a. Amount of understatement on returns with understatement as a percentage of total that should have been reported.
b. Number of returns understating the receipt as a percentage of number of returns that should have reported the item.
SOURCE: Internal Revenue Service, Taxpayer Compliance Measurement Program for 1982 Returns, table 10.

complete audit. In some cases, the purported underreporting of income results from the transmission of the correct dollar amount on the wrong line of the tax return. Moreover, because of our concern with noncompliance and enforcement, the numbers shown here reflect underreporting of income. To the extent that Congress is concerned with the target efficiency of a program, errors resulting from overstating income (or understating deductions and credits) should also be examined.

What the tables do suggest rather strongly is that some areas of the tax code may not be administrable no matter what the level of IRS enforcement resources. The quality of any program run by the government—regardless of whether the program is run through the tax code or through direct expenditure agencies—depends in part upon whether the dollars spent or collected are given to or taken from the persons who were targeted. Only small amounts of inefficiency and error should be allowed. If enforcement efforts are not viable, then policy solutions should be considered.

While it is not my purpose to propose policy solutions to each of these separate enforcement problems, the types of solutions vary widely. One alternative that must be considered is the simple elimination of any credit, deduction, or exemption that is difficult to administer. Recent tax reform proposals, for instance, include an elimination of the political contributions credit (although many of those contributions will still be deductible).

Redesign is also possible. For example, the large error rate in the exemption for parents is due in part to a complicated support test that is hard to calculate and difficult to understand. Simpler support rules—provision of some minimum amount of money or actual residence in the home of the taxpayer—may be preferable. If the government wants to encourage the support of parents, it must also determine whether a given tax provision is the best means of accomplishing the goal, or whether the money might be better spent on direct welfare for elderly poor. Finally, the tax or expenditure program could be designed to spend the allocated revenue in a program designed to minimize error and noncompliance.

Better record keeping or reporting on the part of taxpayers would also improve compliance. In 1982 Congress required certain minimum reporting of tip income by employers. According to separate estimates, this requirement almost doubled the amount of tip income reported between 1982 and 1983 from 16 percent to over 32 percent of total tip income.[4] (Note again that total noncompliance is greater than can be detected through TCMP audits, as reflected in table 4–2.) The error rates are still large enough that these minimum reporting requirements need further examination.

Sometimes a combination of approaches can reduce errors. In the case of the exemption for dependent parents, the Senate recently passed a provision that would require the reporting of social security numbers for virtually all dependents. The IRS would then run a computer check with the Social Security Administration to see if payments from that agency to claimed dependents were so high that dependency would be unlikely. If combined with a support test that was easier to understand, the error rate would probably decrease substantially.

Many policy solutions require some arbitrariness. For car and truck expenses, for instance, one solution would be simply to allow some precise percentage (perhaps 100 percent) of expenses to be written off, even for vehicles with some minimum amount of personal use—for example, for a truck owned by a farmer—as long as the vehicle's primary use is for business. Alternatively, the code could require that persons with two primary places of business—for example, a doctor with an office and a primary hospital—would not be allowed to write off car expenses any more than would a worker with one primary business residence but with a long commute. Each rule would be somewhat arbitrary, but an arbitrary and administrable rule is often preferable to one that appears to be more fair but that cannot be enforced.

Congress and the executive branch at times tackle these administrative problems, but the process remains unsystematic and random. Only the recent budget and tax reform pressures have led to greater consideration of administrative and compliance issues. My proposal would take advantage of this current momentum and set up a systematic method of examining administrative problems within every program run by the IRS, perhaps on some multiyear cycle. Even small programs with little revenue consequence, but large error rates, would be examined. By setting up a systematic approach, consideration would also be required of politically sensitive programs protected by interest groups that want neither greater enforcement nor policy change.

Allocating Resources within the IRS

Unlike most business executives, IRS administrators do not have the authority to spend their funds in ways they consider most likely to accomplish the organizational goals. They are constrained by government-wide rules that determine salary rates for certain personnel, entry levels for other personnel, caps on salaries for top managers, and the extent to which individuals must move into management positions to obtain higher pay or grade levels.

Almost all large organizations, of course, have some rules regarding pay scales, work conditions, and relationships among employees. When those rules cause problems in the operation of the organizations, alternative mechanisms are likely to be developed and new rules adopted. The following facts and circumstances, however, indicate that all problems within the IRS have not been adequately resolved:

- Service centers within the IRS have recently had difficulty attracting new employees and retaining experienced employees. According to one GAO official, "Service Center officials attribute this to such things as the lack of part-time work and flexible work hours at the centers, job stress due to performance standards, and entry level salaries that were often lower than those offered by local fast food restaurants."[5]
- Part of the IRS workload is cyclical, with heavy demand during tax filing season for taxpayer service and for the processing of tax returns. Some IRS officials claim that the quality of applicants for the additional part-time work during tax season has declined. This decline is attributable in part to the increase in the number of married couples working full time and to the increased work opportunities available to women. In effect, cheap labor is no longer available, but pay rates do not reflect the change in circumstances.
- Although the IRS makes heavy use of accountants to perform a variety of functions, including the examination of tax returns, there is a significant gap between government and private sector accounting salaries. One recent study found that salary differentials between the public and private sectors in 1984 were between 33 percent and 40 percent (or between $10,000 and $20,000) for high-rated government positions (GS13-GS15), but significant differences were present at all position levels.[6] Although entry-level positions were filled, attracting top graduates was found to be difficult.
- The IRS, as well as other governmental agencies, has almost no chance of hiring computer science majors out of college. One recent job-market analysis indicated that the entry level salary for computer science majors with no job experience was $23,500, while government entry level salaries were between $13,903 and $17,221. One computer division (dealing with computer hardware) had 213 employees, only one of whom had a bachelor's degree in computer science, although

four others held advanced degrees in information systems and technology.[7]

- To solve difficult technical problems, skilled analysts and programmers are often required. Government-wide personnel rules, however, often require movement into management as a condition of attaining a higher grade. As a result, highly competent programmers and accountants often move on to management positions even if their skills in handling difficult programming and accounting issues could have proved more valuable.

- Some problems interact. Computer specialists, like all professionals, want to develop their skills to the fullest. IRS computer specialists chose antiquated technology as one of the three most important reasons for their planning to leave the IRS in the future.[8]

- A study being conducted at the American Bar Foundation finds that private tax practitioners cite high attrition rates for IRS employees as a major source of problems. Private tax attorneys and accountants also complain that IRS employees are not adequately trained in the tax law, are not technically competent in their area of expertise, or are not familiar with changes in the statutes.[9]

- Although difficult to verify empirically, some officials believe that the continual lowering of maximum federal salaries relative to salaries available in the private sector, combined with the degradation of the value of public service, is eventually going to have a significant effect on the quality of the work performed by the IRS.

The IRS uses several methods to deal with these employment problems. The agency may hire outside consultants for some services, in effect paying additional money for expertise that does not exist internally. For competent junior personnel already hired, it may be possible to grant rapid advancement to make up for differentials in wage rates between the private and public sectors. Because of the large turnover of trained personnel in the service centers, the IRS devotes a large amount of resources to training. Since the IRS has little ability to hire programmers from outside, it trains as programmers many secretaries, tax examiners, and others within the agency who view a career switch as an opportunity for advancement. The typical top-level IRS manager is an intelligent, diligent person from a lesser-known college or university who rose in the ranks through hard work and dedication to public service. Very few high-level managers were graduates of the most famous universities or had been hired from private firms.

Although the IRS's methods of meeting employment needs are at times ingenious, it is not always clear that they are as cost effective as the denied alternatives. The additional training and turnover costs are high. For a variety of reasons, including lack of experience and familiarity, private contractors often impose greater costs on the government than would trained inhouse personnel. The dependence upon internal career development enhances the experience of IRS managers, but denies to the organization some of the expertise, stimuli, and sources of knowledge available to those who may have approached related problems in a different way in the private sector.

Many of the recently documented IRS problems—in the service centers, in posting records accurately, in the computer replacement program—reflect the ways the IRS has been forced to allocate resources over the years.[10] One cannot expect to eliminate all administrative problems, but they can often be mitigated when high-quality personnel and equipment are present throughout an organization. It is my belief that these problems would not have reached a critical state if recent IRS commissioners had been given greater authority to allocate existing resources and personnel in ways that they deemed necessary.

As evidence, first, the IRS had been trying to replace and improve its computer system for years. It recognized the need for upgrading and replacement since the late 1960s. Denial of the right to spend funds for new computers, together with a replacement process that was minimally funded, meant that too much was attempted too late, too hurriedly, and with too little money. In addition, by the time the IRS decided that the capacity of the replacement system was inadequate, the manufacturer had stopped producing the machines the IRS needed because the private sector was already demanding newer, more modern equipment. To compound the problem, the failure to obtain state-of-the-art technology continued to lessen the ability of the IRS to obtain or retain top-quality computer analysts.

Second, the IRS did not support the extent of the cutbacks in taxpayer service personnel. IRS officials were clearly aware of the potential problems that could, and did, arise.

Third, if one reads through the details of problems such as the bad posting of data in the Philadelphia Service Center, what stands out is not so much that errors occurred, or that they might be avoided in the future by implementing more failsafe procedures, but that the errors were correctable at several stages simply through better computer programming.

Finally, some types of problems require the attention not of managers, but simply of top-level analysts, examiners, or programmers. In many parts of the IRS promotion generally requires movement into management positions. For many types of problems, however, good and quick technical thinking—not just better management—may provide solutions.

The commissioner and the assistant commissioners should be given greater leeway to determine spending priorities. If they anticipate computer hardware needs, they should be allowed to plan for those needs and, if necessary, to cover costs by shifting resources, by changing timetables for replacement, or by engaging in forms of capital budgeting. Similarly, they should be given more flexibility to choose between one highly qualified analyst, programmer, accountant, or worker and two moderately qualified persons, and vice-versa. These issues go beyond the IRS, of course. If government personnel policies prevent the hiring of persons with computer science degrees, for example, the IRS can do little about the problem by itself.

The degree of discretion needed may not be great relative to total IRS resources. Nonetheless, organization theory holds that managers need some minimum amount of flexibility and slack to deal with situations that cannot be handled under standard rules or existing organizational modes. If overall salaries for programmers are not increased, for instance, the IRS will still have to rely mainly on individuals who start out with much less training and education in computer science. The resulting problems might be alleviated through fallback approaches, such as strategic placing of, say, fifty very highly qualified, highly paid programmers who are flexible enough to deal with emergencies and difficult programming tasks.

The Congress and the public demand high-quality service and advice from the IRS. The coming of the computer age and the increased complexity of the tax code have intensified the need for trained and professional workers within the IRS. At the same time, pressures to keep down government costs greatly limit the agency's ability to compete with the private sector for individuals with various levels of training or experience. A partial solution to this dilemma is to give greater flexibility to administrators to spend money on those areas with the greatest needs or the best opportunities for marginal improvement.

Other Approaches

Other approaches to improving compliance have been suggested over time. Approaches discussed here include reductions in tax rates, changes in the penalty structure, attempts to affect taxpayer expectations, and further coordination with state and local governments.

Reductions in Tax Rates. When voluntary reporting rates remain constant, a reduction in tax rates simultaneously reduces the amount of underpaid tax. Tax revenues, however, pay for government goods and services. If the levels of those goods and services do not change, then reductions in tax rates only add to budget deficits and lead to higher rates in the future. Moreover, if decreases in income taxes are offset by increases in other taxes, improved compliance in one area may only be offset by decreased compliance elsewhere. Indeed, given the IRS's limited ability to audit taxpayers, expansion of its role to administer more taxes could easily reduce its overall effectiveness and thereby increase noncompliance. Thus, while improved compliance with the tax system may result from an overall reduction in the role of the government and the permanent reduction in tax rates thereby allowed, a reduction in tax rates per se has no such consequence.

Lowering of tax rates, of course, might additionally improve the ratio of reported to unreported income, as underreporting seems to be sensitive to tax rates.[11] The degree of improvement, though, is modest relative to the revenue loss involved. The value of rate reduction again must be judged mainly on grounds other than improvement in tax compliance.

When rate reduction is combined with some types of tax reform, however, there is a multiplier effect on improved compliance. The revenue gained from the elimination of some deduction or credit, for instance, may be used to finance rate reduction on other income. In that case, compliance is improved in three ways: (1) there is no longer any overstatement of the amount to be deducted; (2) the tax owed on other underreported income may be less; and (3) the decrease in the reward for cheating (through tax rate reduction) may further lower the amount of income that is underreported. Thus, the program approach advocated in the first section of this chapter, when it can be combined with rate reduction, provides a useful means of improving tax compliance.

Changes in the Penalty Structure. For the taxpayer, the average or expected cost of a decision not to comply with the tax code depends upon both the probability of being detected and the size of the penalty to be paid. In the United States, as in almost all other countries, penalties for tax cheating are fairly low and imprisonment is rarely used.[12] In the United States the penalty is often only a small percentage of the tax underpayment even when the chance of being detected through audit may be virtually nil. In effect, the expected or average benefits from many types of noncompliance are far in excess of the expected or average costs.

On efficiency grounds alone, increased penalties may be preferable to increased enforcement efforts because only the latter involve the social costs associated with more enforcement personnel and more time spent by taxpayers in audit sessions. The choice of penalty structure, however, is dominated more by equity than by efficiency considerations.

Low penalties reflect a social view that only light fines or no penalties at all are appropriate for many types of tax underpayment. "[S]urveys confirm the view that many taxpayers believe minor tax fiddling to be a widespread and not particularly serious crime, roughly on a par with bicycle theft or stealing from 'a giant corporation.'"[13]

This is not an unusual problem in law enforcement. Equity considerations usually require that the "punishment fit the crime" and that large penalties not be associated with small crimes or misdemeanors, no matter what the effect on deterrence. For instance, only small penalties apply to littering, despite the potential antilitter effect of more severe punishment.

Before 1982, penalties for many types of underreporting were quite low, and interest rates charged on "borrowing" from the U.S. government were often below market interest rates. Various changes in the tax laws in 1982, 1984, and 1986 have changed that situation. Despite concern with particular provisions, tax administrators generally expressed a belief that the penalty structure had been strengthened to a reasonable level. Therefore, while changes in the penalty structure are recognized as options for possibly improving compliance, no recommendations are made here.

Taxpayer Knowledge and Expectations. One of the most useful, yet unmeasurable, ways to affect compliance is through information channels. Taxpayers' expectations are an important determinant of how they behave. Taxpayer services, for example, can reduce taxpayer error by providing greater certainty as to the meaning of the law and its application in particular cases.[14]

Another obvious example is audit. The higher the rate of expected audit, the less likely are taxpayers to underreport their income. As the IRS shifts its resources to cover different compliance problems, it can affect expectations by announcing its efforts. Such warnings, in fact, should be a standard part of IRS outreach.

To attach more social approbation to cheating on tax returns, the IRS could make greater efforts to inform compliant taxpayers that their relative tax burden goes up when underreporting increases. Individuals who find little wrong with taking from big corporations or from big government will likely be much more concerned if they understand the ways they themselves are directly affected when others cheat. A similar problem arises in insurance, where many persons seem to be unaware that unusually large liability awards raise their own premiums for insurance. As pollsters and others know, the method by which information is presented can have a profound difference on a person's reaction to the same set of underlying facts.

The IRS might also encourage compliance by publicizing some of its enforcement activities. Since the IRS has a program to deal with fraudulent tax preparers, it might warn taxpayers that the use of such preparers may increase the probability of audit. Taxpayers would then make greater efforts to seek reputable preparers, while preparers themselves might feel more obligated to advertise themselves as reputable. A similar reinforcing mechanism might be applied to the accurate preparation of returns. In deciding which returns should be audited, the IRS will often let an examiner weed out returns that are less likely to have an audit change. The examiner's selection process is almost surely related to the quality of information provided on the return itself. In choosing between two returns with large noncash charitable contributions, for example, the examiner is more likely to select the return that discloses the least evidence that the valuation was accurate. By letting taxpayers know that well-documented returns are less likely to be audited, honest taxpayers will take more care in the preparation of their returns. Greater care on their part will in turn make easier the identification of noncompliant taxpayers.

Further Coordination with State and Local Governments. One method of increasing the level of penalty expected by persons underreporting income would be to increase the coordination among various tax jurisdictions.[15] If underreporters face a higher probability of paying penalties at any level of government, all levels will likely benefit because of the effect on induced compliance.

One author found that at the state level, "In the majority of states, legislators and administrators have yet to be convinced of the contribution that research, statistical budgeting, and planning activities at the agency level can make to (a) more efficient and equitable allocation of administrative resources and (b) more informed state policy."[16] At the federal level, however, there is inadequate recognition of how improved state administration can increase levels of compliance with the federal laws.

One difficulty is that increased federal efforts to help the states could actually decrease the measured level of enforcement revenues gained by the federal government. Here is a classic case of a social problem in which the social benefits of cooperation do not necessarily accrue to those doing the cooperation. If the marginal improvement in compliance is greater for aiding federal-state cooperation than for increasing audit coverage at the federal level, then revenues spent in the former pursuit are more cost effective.

Efforts at federal-state cooperation have improved over the years, and all states make some effort to use information available from the federal government. This study has only touched upon the issue, but it appears that much can still be done.[17] No matter who pays for the efforts, they would likely be quite cost-effective.

In summary, there are a variety of ways, short of increased resources, to improve compliance with the tax laws. Many, such as changes in tax policies and reductions in the number of programs run through the IRS, require congressional approval. Others require greater allocational authority to the IRS for acquiring proper equipment and needed personnel. Finally, many other approaches offer the potential of at least modest improvement in levels of compliance. None of these approaches, however, can eliminate the need to audit those items of income and expense that can be checked only through an audit process.

Notes

1. There are other reasons as well. Additional deductions and credits put into the tax code do not show up as governmental expenditures; hence, their true cost is more hidden.

2. Office of the Secretary, U.S. Department of the Treasury, *Tax Reform for Fairness, Simplicity and Economic Growth* (Washington, D.C.: Superintendent of Documents, 1984).

3. When the amount that should be reported is small relative to under- and overreporting, the error rates may seem unusually large. In the case of total rental and royalty income, for example, the amount that should have been reported ($4.13 billion) equaled the amount actually reported (-$1.25 billion), plus the amount of understatement ($6.36 billion), less the amount of overstatement ($0.98 billion). The amount of understatement was thus greater than the amount that should have been reported, and the error rate (the former divided by the latter) was greater than one.

4. See Jim Dumais, "Impact of TEFRA on Tip Income Reporting," in *1986 Update: Trend Analysis and Related Statistics* (Washington, D.C.: Internal Revenue Service, 1986), pp. 105–10.

5. Statement of Johnny C. Finch, General Accounting Office, Before the Subcommittee on Oversight, Committee on Ways and Means, U.S. House of Representatives, on IRS Service Center Operations, December 16, 1985.

6. ICF Incorporated, "Accountants and Auditors: A Summary of Recent Employment Trends and Forecasts," unpublished manuscript, 1985.

7. Office of Assistant Commissioner (Computer Services), Internal Revenue Service, "Recruitment and Turnover Study," 1984.

8. Ibid.

9. Mary Coyne and Kent Smith, American Bar Foundation, Letter to the Section on Taxation of the American Bar Association, February 11, 1986.

10. These problems were discussed at the end of chapter 2.

11. See Charles T. Clotfelter, "Tax Evasion and Tax Rates: An Analysis of Individual Returns," *Review of Economics and Statistics* 3 (1983), pp. 363–73.

12. Nathan Boidman, "A Summary of What Can Be Learned from the Experience of Other Countries with Income Tax Compliance Problems," 37 Bulletin for International Fiscal Documentation 415 (1983).

13. James S. Henry, "Noncompliance with the U.S. Tax Law— Evidence on Size, Growth, and Composition," in *Income Tax Compliance* (American Bar Association, 1983), p. 54.

14. See, for instance, John T. Scholz, "Coping With Complexity: A Bounded Rationality Perspective on Taxpayer Compliance," *Proceedings of the Seventy-eighth Annual Conference of the National Tax Association—Tax Institute of America* (NTA, 1985), pp.30–38.

15. The General Accounting Office recently gave new impetus to efforts at federal-state cooperation. See General Accounting Office, "The Federal-State Tax Information Exchange Program," Washington, D.C.: General Accounting Office, December 1985.

16. See Clara Penniman, *State Income Taxation* (Baltimore, Md.: The Johns Hopkins University Press, 1980), pp. 128–29.

17. For a comprehensive review of the mutual financing issues facing federal, state, and local governments, see George F. Break, *Financing Government in a Federal System* (Washington, D.C.: The Brookings Institution, 1980).

5
The Budget Process

Previous chapters have been concerned mainly with enforcement efforts and with other ways of improving compliance with the tax laws. Stress has been placed on developing a decision-making process that allows policy makers fundamental consideration of all social benefits and costs of alternative actions. This chapter deals with the budget process itself and points out the inadequacies of that process for making decisions on financing tax administration.

Summary of the Process

At any given time, the IRS may be involved in budgeting for three different years. IRS executives and staff begin planning for a new budget about twenty months before the start of each fiscal year. Each assistant commissioner and the chief counsel develop budget proposals for their functional areas, based in part on research devoted to projecting future numbers of returns and other measures of workload. The Finance Division next coordinates the initial budget proposals and provides related cost estimates. Because many activities are interrelated, coordinated planning is required. Marginal yield-to-cost ratios are estimated for changes in different activities, and a resource allocation model is used to identify the costs and revenues of enforcement efforts on a year-by-year basis.

Following review and setting of priorities by the commissioner and other senior officials, the IRS submits its budget request to Treasury in June. Treasury, in turn, spends the summer reviewing the IRS request, as well as requests from other Treasury agencies and offices. In September the complete Treasury budget request is submitted to the Office of Management and Budget.

In January of the following year, the president's budget message, including a recommended budget for the IRS, is submitted to Congress. In the succeeding months, hearings are held by the House and Senate appropriations committees, by the oversight subcommittees of the House Committee on Ways and Means and the Senate Finance Committee, and occasionally by the government operations committees. While the appropriations committees set overall levels of staffing and funding for the IRS, the tax-writing committees are charged with raising various levels of revenue under the budget process.

During the summer, the Congress marks up the budget in anticipation of making some final decisions. Although the congressional budget process was designed to make annual appropriations for administrative agencies, the IRS since 1981 has not had a regular appropriations act and has been operating under continuing resolutions (in fiscal 1983, there were four separate continuing resolutions). Appropriations are set in four separate accounts: processing tax returns; examination and appeals; investigation, collection and taxpayer service; and other salaries and expenses. The last is small, and the total IRS budget is divided in roughly equal shares among the first three. The commissioner has very limited flexibility to shift money among these four accounts or even among programs within each account. Supplemental appropriations requests are often submitted to deal with changes in pay costs, major tax legislation, and administrative problems.

Table 5–1 summarizes in staff years the resource levels requested and allowed at various stages of the budget process. The original IRS submission to Treasury varies widely from year to year, probably reflecting different perceptions of optimal budget strategy as much as changes in the agency's actual needs. As can be seen in the table, however, the final allowances for staff years seem to be determined mainly by decisions made within the executive branch by Treasury and OMB. Although congressional review may often be thorough, ultimate congressional action seldom results in a budget appropriation that differs greatly from what the president requests.

Determinants of Spending Levels

Although an ideal budget process would be driven by a consideration of all the benefits and costs associated with different levels of IRS funding, three factors seem to have dominated the decision-making process. In areas such as returns processing and taxpayer service, public reaction seems to be the prime determinant of staff levels. As long as refund checks are sent on time and taxpayers can obtain some minimum amount of guidance through phone calls or other contacts with the IRS, Congress and OMB seem satisfied. OMB frequently suggests cutting personnel for these types of functions *until* the public complains or public attention is drawn to a particular problem. In

TABLE 5–1
BUDGET SUBMISSIONS FOR THE INTERNAL REVENUE SERVICE, FISCAL YEARS 1974–1985
(thousands of staff years)

Fiscal Year	Treasury Submission	Effect of Executive Branch Review					Effect of Legislative Branch Review	
		Treasury Allowance	OMB Submission	OMB Allowance	Congressional Budget	Congressional Budget vs. Treasury Submission	Congressional Action	Action vs. Congressional Budget
1974	85.9	−7.3%	79.6	−6.0%	74.8	−12.9%	75.9	+1.5%
1975	92.5	−7.6%	85.5	−3.7%	82.3	−11.1%	82.3	
1976	96.6	−4.9%	91.8	−8.1%	84.4	−12.6%	84.2	−.3%
1977	100.1	−5.9%	94.1	−13.4%	81.6	−18.5%	81.7	+.1%
1978	85.6	−1.0%	84.7	−.3%	84.5	−1.3%	84.2	−.4%
1979	93.8	−1.8%	92.2	−6.1%	86.5	−7.8%	86.5	
1980	96.0	−7.5%	88.9	−1.8%	87.2	−9.2%	88.2	+1.1%
1981	95.5	−2.2%	93.4	−6.2%	87.7	−8.2%	87.7	
1982	101.4	−8.1%	93.2	−9.9%	83.9	−17.2%	84.4	+.5%
1983	92.8	−8.1%	85.3	+3.9%	88.7	−4.4%	90.4	+1.9%
1984	97.5	−8.2%	89.5	+2.5%	91.8	−5.9%	89.3	−2.7%
1985	95.5	−2.8%	92.8	−4.8%	88.4	−7.4%	87.7	−0.7%

SOURCE: Internal Revenue Service.

1985, for instance, the IRS's failure to return many refund checks within a reasonable time, combined with the associated increase in correspondence from taxpayers, led to congressional pressures to increase staffing.

For most of the postwar era, a second factor affecting IRS resources has been limits on the size of the federal government, as measured by the number of its employees. Numerous interviews with both budget and IRS officials make clear that this concern has tended to override almost every other consideration. The IRS competes in its budget process with other agencies seeking funds. Every president in modern history has been committed to increasing expenditures for favored activities or pet projects, whether social security, defense or welfare, and simultaneously to reducing costs and limiting government growth.

When a president attempts to contain the size of government, he often first asks OMB for cutbacks in personnel.[1] Although the Treasury Department is run rather leanly, the secretary of the treasury often regards himself as the chief economic spokesperson for the executive branch and, therefore, feels a need to lead the way in showing that such economies can be found. Since the IRS has such a large proportion of total Treasury staff, Treasury leadership necessarily entails reductions in the number of persons working for the IRS.

Even within the government at large, the IRS is a major user of staff resources. Secretaries of the Treasury have historically grown weary of their limited role in temporary crusades to reduce the level of federal employment, and the IRS was often able to convince them that increased levels of enforcement activity would be an economical way to increase revenues and reduce the deficit without raising taxes. The secretaries then supported these arguments by submitting requests to the president for additional appropriations for tax administration. Concern that these changes would add to the total number of federal employees, however, still usually deterred presidential action.[2] In one case in the late 1970s, for instance, the president backed away from any action once he was reminded that increases in IRS personnel would make more difficult the attainment of total federal employment goals.

Recently, concern over the budget deficit and with providing money for tax reform has made important a third factor: short-term boosts in revenues through increased enforcement and collection activity. Since substantial budget deficits are now projected to last for many years, this third factor could become dominant in the late 1980s.

The congressional budget process, however, has had difficulty dealing with the new shift in emphasis. Decisions on spending and revenues are made independently in separate committees. The means of financing increased enforcement activity must come from the appropriations committees. These committees, however, are usually charged with limiting total expenses and cannot be credited with net gains in revenues. The tax-writing committees, on the other hand, cannot change appropriations levels in order to use enforcement activity as an alternative to tax increases. This dilemma has caused jurisdictional disputes between the committees and has hampered decision making.

In 1986 the Senate Finance Committee unsuccessfully tried to attach a provision on IRS funding to tax reform. The agency's resources would have been increased without going through the normal budget process. Technically, a trust fund was to be set up; but the actual effect would have been to set IRS levels of funding for five years. The approach of the Senate Finance Committee solved two procedural problems: it allowed the tax-writing committees to avoid the congressional appropriations process for five years, and it allowed the tax reform bill to lay claim to revenue gains from appropriations that otherwise would be decided several years in the future. OMB opposed the provision as an unhealthy precedent in the appropriations process; in addition, the revenues to be gained from increased enforcement had already been proposed for deficit reduction and could not be spent again for tax reform.

Budget Cycles

The ups and downs of IRS staffing, and the 180-degree shifts of opinion by Congress and the administration on whether to increase or decrease the size of the IRS, are reflected in the budget changes of the 1980s. In the early 1980s there was a substantial push for staff decreases; as a result, between 1980 and 1982 there was a net cutback of over 4,500 staff years, or over 5 percent of total personnel. In 1984 a large reduction in returns-processing personnel was also achieved, but was immediately countered in the following years with increases to overcome the resulting difficulties. Similarly, the number of revenue agents and tax auditors declined by over 8½ percent between 1980 and 1984, a drop that was more than offset by proposed increases for 1986 and beyond.

Not only is there a multiyear cycle of ups and downs, but also for each fiscal year the amount of revenue available to administrators varies widely over the budget planning season. Figure 5–1 shows some details for fiscal year 1986. Because of federal deficit problems, in late 1984 and early 1985 OMB supported a movement toward austerity

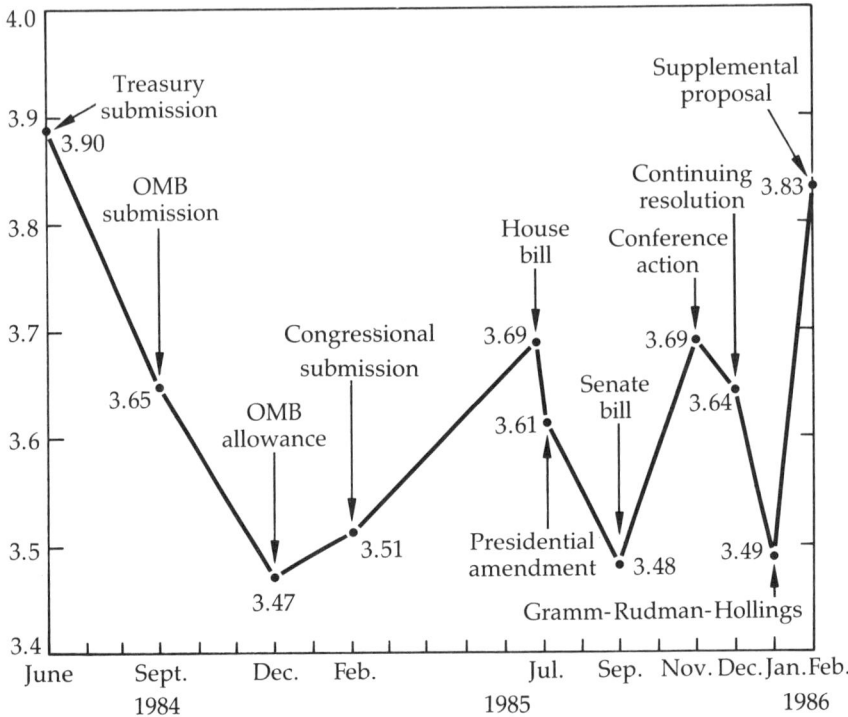

FIGURE 5–1
FY 1986 BUDGET HISTORY
(billions of dollars)

SOURCE: Internal Revenue Service.

and reductions in many IRS functions. By mid-1985, the 1985 filing problems for 1984 returns had come to light, and momentum built for a higher level of funding. By the time of a continuing resolution in late 1985, funding was set near the original level proposed by Treasury to OMB. The Gramm-Rudman-Hollings Act then forced another decrease on the IRS, but a supplemental request was proposed to increase funding by $340 million, almost half of which is being used to offset reductions from the Gramm-Rudman-Hollings Act. As indicated before, the IRS eventually felt that it had to operate under the assumption that the supplemental amount would be approved, even though technically only a virtually impossible series of layoffs could have allowed existing legal appropriations limits to be met.

By the time that the FY 1987 budget was submitted, revenue considerations led to additional proposals for increased IRS staffing.

Not only did the administration submit a fiscal 1987 revenue initiative to increase funding for the IRS, but congressional tax reform proposals also began to use additional enforcement revenues as a mechanism for raising revenues to pay for reform.

Some Difficulties

The existing budget process results in both poor policy and inefficient administrative planning. Policy with respect to IRS appropriations is guided not by comparisons of social benefits and social costs, but by the effects of IRS activity on a single parameter. For many years, that parameter was total federal employment. More recently, it has been revenues from enforcement. Both are simplistic and often misleading measures of the effects of changing levels of IRS resources.

Some IRS problems are directly traceable to this budgetary process. The IRS shifts resources more rapidly than necessary and then incurs additional costs by trying to correct the resulting problems. Recruitment is hindered because available resource levels are often unknown, and potential employees are unwilling to risk employment on the chance that budget authority might be obtained.[3] The lack of a firm budget requires planning for multiple contingencies; the time could be spent better on internal administrative and operational matters. Instead of planning how to write better regulations or how to improve enforcement activity, enormous efforts are wasted in trying to accommodate increases and decreases in available resources.

The IRS cannot develop a long-term plan because it would quickly become obsolete in this type of budgetary environment. Even if the agency would adopt a plan, many options are foreclosed because of the accounting methods used for government budgetary purposes. One example that stands out is the lack of capital budgeting to deal with computer replacement and enhancement. Other long-term planning is discouraged because the ultimate results—a better administration several years down the road—have no effect upon the parameters of concern to the policy makers: near-term government employment levels and budget deficits.

The recent attention paid to IRS enforcement as a way to deal with budget deficits and to pay for tax reform has been accompanied by a lack of understanding of the meaning of related revenue figures. Quickly forgotten is that total revenues are dependent upon total compliance, not upon the dollar amount of enforcement revenue collected. Thus, cost-effective ways of improving compliance may depend upon hard-to-measure increases in compliance which are independent of direct enforcement yields.

Another difficulty arises because budget accounting is done essentially on a cash-flow basis rather than according to the present value of changes in revenues and expenditures. Gains from many long-term projects often occur after the five-year planning period, but costs occur sooner. Some revenue gains, on the other hand, are overstated in the short run. For instance, recent estimates of increased revenues from expanded IRS resources include more timely payments due to increased collections from accounts receivable. To the extent that those payments would have been made eventually, the estimate of revenue increases over the next few years clearly overstates the long-term gains to the federal government.

The process of estimating revenues also results in some double counting. When there is a decrease in IRS resources, the budget has not contained an estimate of revenue loss. When there is an increase, in part simply to replace resources that were lost earlier, a revenue yield is estimated. Moreover, estimates of revenue collections independent of policy changes are projected on the basis of historical patterns, which include improvements in efficiency within the IRS. To the extent that a supplemental appropriations request fully counts those efficiency gains as due to the appropriations, there is an overstatement of the net increase in revenues.

One difficulty is that there is no established or agreed-upon baseline from which to make estimates. One might assume, for example, that the IRS operates at current staffing levels, that some redirection of resources will take place automatically, and that some improvement in revenue yields would occur simply from those reallocations and from other improvements in efficiency. Further increases or decreases in revenue yields can then be predicted by changing resources relative to that baseline. Without a consistent baseline, minor changes in assumptions—for instance, as to the audit rate for large corporations—can have a substantial influence on revenue estimates and on estimates of marginal changes in yield to cost. What needs to be carried forward to the budget process are the estimates both of losses due to declines in staffing and of gains due to increases. Ordinary efficiency gains due to better optimization at existing levels of resources should be understood to be counted at least partially in the existing revenue estimating process.

Toward a Solution

Although waste and inefficiency inevitably result from the existing budget process, the IRS's problems cannot be considered in isolation. Other policies, programs, and administrative agencies are affected by the short-term accounting horizon and by the failure to weigh more carefully social benefits and costs.

Although this study does not address the government budget process per se, the IRS presents a case study of an agency with problems that could have been avoided if a better process had been in place. A minimal list of improvements includes the following:

• longer-term accounting of benefits and costs of changes in both policy and in appropriations for administration. Ideally, the accounting would also be done on a present value basis;

• consistent accounting on the up-side and down-side of various changes in appropriations and policies;

• assignment of responsibility for the revenue effects of appropriations to the committee given authority over those appropriations (this need not be the appropriations committees); at the same time, fuller accounting of the administrative costs of various policies;

• some movement toward capital accounting in the budget. Even if done on only a minor scale, agencies should be able to better plan for items such as computer replacement and enhancement;

• longer-term planning cycles, at least for administrative agencies. Multiyear budgeting need not apply equally to all agencies and programs, and supplemental changes in appropriation levels can always be proposed.

Notes

1. As John Scholz states, "In OMB and Congressional appropriations committees . . . the dominant concern has been in making 'equitable' cuts for all agencies to reach spending targets set at a different level." See John T. Scholz, "Political Context of Tax Administration," paper presented at the Symposium on Taxpayer Compliance Research, January 15–17, 1986, Padre Island, Texas.

2. Jerome Kurtz, former commissioner of the Internal Revenue Service (1977-1980), argues, "The only reason that I can see to limit IRS is the political importance that is placed on the total number of Federal employees. That has a certain magic to it and winds up lumping IRS in with everyone else. The problem basically is that the IRS is labor intensive; 75 or 80 percent of the IRS's total budget is payroll. So when you talk about increasing Internal Revenue Service resources, you are talking about increasing people." See *Administration's Fiscal Year 1982 Budget Proposals Relating to Staffing of the Internal Revenue Service*, Hearings Before the Subcommittee on Oversight of the Committee on Ways and Means, U.S. House of Representatives, May 11, 1981 (Washington, D.C.: Government Printing Office, 1981).

3. See William E. Williams, "Strengthening IRS Examination and Collection Processes by Administrative Changes in Staffing, Training, Deployment and Technology," *Income Tax Compliance* (American Bar Association, 1983), p. 246.

6
Summary and Conclusions

The Internal Revenue Service administers many, if not most, of the economic policies of the United States government. From one perspective, this agency is in charge not only of the revenue side of the budget, but also of a large portion of the expenditure side. The numerous deductions, exclusions, exemptions, and credits in the tax code are essentially programs designed to promote saving, investment, housing, medical care, and other social objectives. Total IRS costs of administering these revenue and expenditure programs is about one-half of 1 percent of net revenues, about the same percentage as in the late 1940s, although the trend in the past two decades has been slightly upward. Over the same period, IRS resources have probably fallen relative to workload, as measured by the complexity of the tax code, number of returns, and requests for taxpayer service.

The efficiency of the Service has been enhanced over the years, in part because of improvements in computer technology, the increased number of information reports received, and reallocations of personnel. Along with an expanded capacity to detect underreporting of such items as wages, interest, dividends, and capital gains, however, has come a lower rate of audit for many deductions and sources of income that are subject to neither withholding nor information reporting. Noncompliance remains significant and has probably been encouraged by recent declines in the percentage of returns that are audited. In the past few years, the IRS has also suffered from problems with respect to the timing and procedure for computer replacement, delays in mailing refund checks, improper posting of data, increases in accounts receivable, dedication of a large percentage of staff to tax shelters, and, simultaneously, the lack of a firm long-term or short-term budget by which to plan.

One way to deal with these problems of tax administration and compliance is to augment the resources available to the IRS. Based upon several analyses—a review of historical experience, extrapolation of marginal yields expected from examination, and regressions relating budget costs to enforcement revenues from examination—it seems safe to say that even with significant increases in the IRS budget, the revenue yield will still be a multiple of the costs incurred.

At 1985 staffing levels of the examination division alone, marginal yields to costs for many types of returns fall in the four-to-one to seven-to-one range. Even if the examination staff were to be enlarged by 60 percent over 1985 levels—that is, increased by 15,000 personnel —marginal yields to costs for *additional examination* of most classes of returns would still range between two-to-one and three-to-one. That level of staff increase, however, is more than twice what has been proposed in recent budget submissions and is greater than the examination division could accommodate in any short period of time. Moreover, this estimate represents a lower bound on possible revenue yield from additional IRS efforts, for higher returns are often available from other activities within the examination division and outside of it. New and efficient programs are also constantly being developed. At the end of 1985, for example, additional resources could be used most effectively for such items as the processing of additional information returns and the reduction in accounts receivable.

Still, one must be careful in implementing any policy to add to IRS resources. Marginal yields decline as existing activities are expanded, and it is dangerous to extrapolate too far beyond experience. Since the most cost-effective increases in compliance often result from the adoption of new techniques, not from the expansion of existing activity, a separate assessment of each of these techniques has to be made as they become available. Regardless of the direct enforcement revenue that may be generated, however, additional examinations are warranted mainly because the current audit rate is probably too low to provide an adequate disincentive to certain types of noncompliance.

Increases in enforcement activity entail real social costs. These costs include the greater allocation of workers in society to tax enforcement activities and the additional time and energy that taxpayers —compliant as well as noncompliant—must devote to tax concerns. Offsetting these costs in part are efficiency gains, especially from reduction of any tax-induced advantages given in the marketplace to taxpayers who are noncompliant.

The principal advantage of increased enforcement is greater equity in the distribution of tax burdens. When yields exceed costs, tax rates for compliant taxpayers can be reduced. The monetary costs of enforcement, plus the net amount of enforcement revenues over costs, is then paid entirely by noncompliant taxpayers. Even without this net redistribution, society has shown a willingness in all areas of law enforcement, not just in taxation, to pay a reasonable price to ensure that the laws of the country are fairly and equitably enforced. In my view, cost-effective enforcement is preferable to an increase in statutory tax rates; however, the final choice is a societal, not an individual, one.

In addition to increased enforcement, there are alternative ways of improving compliance. Simplification and reduction in the number of programs run by the IRS, enhanced by any rate reduction, would reduce both noncompliance and the cost of enforcing the tax laws. For programs that remain, compliance can often be improved through redesign and through adoption of rules that, although partly arbitrary, are at least enforceable.

Unfortunately, the separation of administration from policy in the executive branch, along with the congressional separation of appropriations from revenue decisions, deflects attention from these policy alternatives and hampers data collection on the operation and results of existing programs. Recent tax reforms, including the major reform effort of 1984-1986, have made some progress toward simplification, but these advances are offset by the imposition of new complexities elsewhere. Although the number of itemizers and taxpayers with positive liability will decline after 1986, for example, new minimum taxes and limitations on loss write-offs will add considerably to the number of taxpayer errors. Past administrative experience with minimum taxes and similar types of provisions is not encouraging.

Some of the IRS's current problems could also be mitigated by granting greater leeway to the commissioner and assistant commissioners to determine how resources should be spent. In the case of computer programmers, accountants, and seasonal workers in some service centers, there is ample documentation that at many levels the IRS does not offer competitive salaries. Resulting difficulties could be moderated if there were greater flexibility to hire the necessary qualified personnel in key functional and geographical areas. The recent decline in the perceived value of public service is also likely to hinder the overall functioning of agencies like the Internal Revenue Service. One is led to recall the effect on the military services of a similar decline in public esteem not many years ago.

Although the measurement of results is often difficult, other factors have a significant influence on taxpayer compliance and on the revenues collected by the federal government. Especially crucial are the ways information is provided to taxpayers and the level of coordination among taxing jurisdictions.

The budget process currently is not designed to make efficient choices on the level of funding for tax administration. Many benefits and costs do not enter into the decision-making process. At times, the process has been driven far too much by the desire to constrain the number of government personnel or to gain additional short-term revenues. In the 1980s, administrative mistakes were inevitable as the IRS was forced first to cut back, then to increase, the number of staff years devoted to various program units. In addition, each year's proposed budget goes through so many changes that managers often do not know whether to plan for increases or decreases in staff levels, operational planning is delayed, recruitment is hampered, and no long-term organizational plan can be developed.

Budget accounting also does not provide for long-term comparisons of benefits and costs. It discourages improvements that entail current costs that will provide long-term benefits. Capital budgeting for such items as computer hardware is denied. Consistent accounting has not yet been achieved to measure the revenue effect of increases or decreases in IRS budgets.

Recommendations

A summary of the recommendations of this study follows:

• Expansion of the resources made available to the Internal Revenue Service seems to be warranted. This expansion should be used in part to finance an increase in examination activity, especially for those receipts or deductions that can be checked only through an audit process. At the same time, collection and other downstream costs of this expansion should be fully budgeted.

• Policy alternatives to enforcement efforts should be given greater consideration. The Congress and the executive branch should study the error rates, target efficiency, costs of auditing, and other administrative aspects of every program that is put into the tax code. These studies must not only outline existing and potential problems, but also investigate both administrative and policy alternatives to deal with the problems. Given the current lack of resources for research on tax policy and administration, simple directives or statements of intention by policy makers will be inadequate. Instead, the studies must be planned, personnel allocated, and a timetable established. Perhaps it would be most useful to start with the programs or provisions for which compliance problems or error rates are greatest. Along with detailed studies, the IRS should publish regularly a list of its most unadministrable programs. By using a criterion such as error rate to determine the components of the list, the problems inherent even in some politically sensitive programs will more likely come to light and be addressed.

- The commissioner and assistant commissioners should be given greater flexibility to allocate resources, especially to hire the necessary qualified personnel in key functional and geographical areas. Some IRS problems raise questions as to the adequacy of government personnel policies. Use of across-the-board, rather than selective, policies to pare personnel costs may actually raise the net costs of certain activities and add to, rather than subtract from, the budget deficit.

- The most cost effective ways to improve compliance are often the least measurable. Although the political process may provide little support, the commissioner must continue to devote considerable effort to improving the ways the IRS provides information to taxpayers and to coordinating with other taxing jurisdictions.

- The budget process for the IRS and other agencies should be changed to provide for: longer-term accounting of benefits and costs; consistent accounting on both the up-side and the down-side of changes in appropriations and policies; responsibility for both appropriations and the revenue effects of those appropriations to reside with the same decision makers (or the same committees in Congress); some capital accounting, at least for such items as computer replacement; and longer-term planning cycles for administrative agencies, perhaps through the selective use of multiyear budgeting.

One final point needs to be made. What is becoming obvious in the case of both budget policy and personnel policy is that blanket, ill-designed cutbacks do not always lower the real cost of government. Revenues and the quality of services sometimes drop by more than the costs saved, and in many cases the cutbacks are quickly overturned once new problems arise. In the case of the IRS, some reductions in resources have decreased net government revenues, and, to the extent that tax rates are thereby kept higher, government intrusion in the economy may actually have increased.

Limiting the administrative cost of government is a difficult task, but it must be handled mainly from the demand, not the supply, side. The administrative and personnel costs of government can be lessened if the number of policies and programs run by the government is reduced, and if the rules are simplified. What will not work well is a simple reduction in the support given to persons who are asked simultaneously to regulate, administer, and enforce an expanding list of programs and policies.

Appendix

Suggested Improvements in IRS Techniques

While conducting this type of study, the investigator will inevitably encounter techniques employed by other researchers that could be improved or tested further. This appendix contains several suggestions to the IRS, especially with regard to the way it allocates enforcement personnel and measures the results of that allocation.

Pension and Other Government Costs. In estimating the costs of examination, the developers of the Examination Model have taken care to incorporate various downstream and support costs such as fringe benefits and staff costs in other divisions such as collection and personnel. Budget accounting within the U.S. government, however, does not attribute to agencies the present value of the expected cost of future pensions. In part, this is because the pension system is not adequately funded to meet future costs. Nonetheless, the failure to add in these government costs may lead policy makers outside the IRS to use yield/cost ratios that understate total social costs. Pension costs, as well as other governmental costs outside the IRS—for example, support personnel within the Office of Personnel Management—must be added to the cost figure presented by the IRS.

Taxpayer Costs. When social benefits and costs are calculated—rather than budget costs alone—the IRS should take into account the time, professional assistance, and other related costs that are imposed upon taxpayers when the rate of audit coverage increases. For taxpayers who are compliant, or whose errors are quite small, these costs are real and should not be ignored. For noncompliant taxpayers, one could consider these additional costs a component of penalties paid. Although the estimates might be crude, the IRS does know the amount of time spent in audit, the income of the audited taxpayer, and other data that could be used in such calculations. Taking these costs into account would also help the IRS demonstrate that concern for the taxpayer is an important part of its decision-making process.

71

Replacement of Average Costs with Marginal Costs. In the estimates of yield-to-cost developed in the Examination Model, the use of an average cost assumption should be abandoned. It should be possible to measure at least the amount of time spent by examiners on returns with different ranges of DIF scores. For instance, those returns in the top 0.5 percent of all DIF scores may take less time to audit than those in the top 0.5–1.0 percent range. They may, however, be more costly to examine because they require the use of more highly qualified or more highly paid personnel. (See Improved Testing of Audit Experience, below.)

Effect of Screener on Yields from Examination. When the IRS selects returns for audit according to DIF scores, not all returns with the highest scores are audited. A "screener" still makes some manual selection of those returns thought most likely to have underpaid tax. Although computer selection is still the primary screening process, the screener may eliminate, say, one-fourth of those returns sent down for examination.

The screener is an important player whose actions can have a significant effect on the ultimate efficiency of the examination process. The IRS has concluded through studies that screeners do indeed aid in the selection of returns with high potential yields. Still, too little is understood about this part of the process. Estimates of the revenues gained through this manual screening process, for example, are not available. Logically, however, they could be large, as the computer cannot determine whether or not returns are well documented.

In calculating the marginal yields from additional examination, the Examination Model should be adjusted to treat the manual screening process more rigorously. Suppose that in a given examination class the top 2 percent of returns are sent down for audit, that one quarter of those returns are weeded out by the screener, and that the rest are audited. The Examination Model currently estimates that the yield from the next return sent down for audit will be similar to that of a return with a DIF score at the top 1½ percentile level rather than at the top 2 percentile level. Although the discounting from TCMP yields to examination yields implicitly takes some of the difference into account, the accuracy of this adjustment cannot be determined without further knowledge of the screener's effectiveness.

Use of Alternative Statistical Techniques. Several times during this study, IRS officials were asked whether regression analysis and other sophisticated statistical techniques might not be used in place of the DIF process. This suggestion has also been made in the past in other studies such as that performed by the National Bureau of Standards.[1] IRS officials reply that they continually test different techniques, but that none has been able to improve upon the results obtained from DIF selection.

No matter what statistical technique is used, it is possible that enough testing has been done over the years that improvements in yields are small. Another reason for changing techniques, however, is the IRS's concern that the DIF formula not be revealed to the public. If continuous variables were to be used, and if all returns were to have some positive probability of audit, the problems of revelation would be reduced considerably. Suppose, for example, that the IRS does not want taxpayers in a given audit class to know that interest deductions between $1,000 and $1,999 are not likely to affect the probability of audit, but that $2,000 to $3,999 of such deductions would increase a DIF score, and probability of audit, significantly. A taxpayer then could lessen greatly the chance of audit simply by reducing deductions by as little as a dollar, from $2,000 to $1,999. With the use of continuous variables, as are commonly used in regressions, no such problem results. Marginal changes of a few dollars in any income or deduction statement will in turn have only a marginal effect on the DIF score.

A Positive Probability of Audit. Closely related to the use of alternative statistical techniques is the development of a method through which all taxpayers have at least some small probability of audit.[2] The IRS partially achieves this goal by dividing taxpayers into various classes and by auditing some fraction of returns in each class. Nonetheless, outside of the TCMP process, within each class most returns have virtually no probability of audit. Since high DIF scores are determined by extraordinary amounts of different income and expense items, those with ordinary amounts simply are not subject to audit, except through other special programs.

The selection process could be altered to ensure that persons with different DIF scores are audited with varying amounts of probability. For instance, no matter what the DIF score, the minimum probability of examination might be set at one quarter of 1 percent. Although direct enforcement yield may decline slightly, compliance (and hence, total revenues) would probably be improved over the long run. Some taxpayers are very risk averse, and at least these taxpayers may be expected to respond significantly to only slight enforcement efforts.

Downstream Effects. Through its work on a comprehensive enforcement resource allocation model, the IRS has considerably improved its ability to estimate the effect of changes in resources in one division upon the workload of other divisions. This improvement in estimation has still not led to optimal planning in the budget process, however, as exemplified in the recent failure to provide for the downstream costs of a proposed increase in examination personnel. More examinations mean more collections and litigation, and all such costs should be recognized. Unfortunately, the budget process does not demand such accounting even when the IRS calculates future costs correctly.

Within the IRS, as noted in the text, enforcement yield from accounts receivable is overstated by the amount of payments that would be made regardless of IRS activity. In some cases, additional enforcement efforts will at first result in accelerated revenue collection, but acceleration per se affects only timing of payments, not the total amount that will be collected. To accommodate these downstream effects on yield, the budget process needs to use present value accounting or long accounting periods.

Estimating Complexity. One of the most difficult tasks for the IRS is measuring the complexity of tax filing. At least one of its current methods is misleading and should be revised. The IRS measures the number of complex returns by standards such as income levels without changing from year to year the nominal income level that divides complex from simple returns. Income growth in the economy, however, could move many taxpayers into the complex category even if there had been no real change in their economic activity or complexity of their returns. The number of lines on a return is not an adequate measure of complexity either, as sometimes additional lines actually make calculations easier for taxpayers who do not understand the law. What might be compared over time are the amount of time spent by taxpayers or tax preparers in filling out their tax returns, the number of special credits, deductions, and special allowances (such as income averaging) taken by taxpayers, and the already available measures of number of tax returns and phone calls to the IRS. Although no one measure is adequate by itself, the IRS should eliminate any measure that is clearly misleading. An additional reason for attention to these measures is that passage of major tax reform demands some long-term accounting of the effects of reform on the complexity of tax filing.

Improved Testing of Audit Experience. Many improvements in the method of selecting returns for audit seem possible if and when the IRS obtains additional computer hardware and software for its examination personnel. There is no reason, for instance, why the curve for audit experience has to be estimated from the TCMP curve, as in figure 3–1. The audit curve could be derived directly if examiners would record appropriate information, including DIF scores and errors in amounts reported by taxpayers for various line items, onto computer files. With the development of appropriate data, it would be possible to test the efficiency of alternative methods of examination. In addition, costs could be related to items examined, DIF scores, and grade of examiner. Marginal cost curves for the Exam Model could then be derived.

As noted in the text, the IRS seems to be several years behind in obtaining computer equipment for many of its personnel. This deficiency is probably due to a budget process that rewards mainly those efforts with measurable short-term results. A multi-year effort is required to provide hardware, software, and training to personnel, to record additional information, and finally to use the additional data generated to test ways of increasing efficiency. The short accounting period of the budget process tends to defer activities with large potential long-term returns.

Notes

1. See Karla L. Hoffman, Lambert S. Joel, and Martin H. Pearl, Center for Applied Mathematics, National Engineering Laboratory, National Bureau of Standards, Washington, D.C., *Resource Requirements and Allocations in IRS Audit Division, Technical Report to the Audit Division, Internal Revenue Services,* February 1979.

2. Kent W. Smith and Karyl A. Kinsey also conclude that "the combined consequence of all selection methods should be that every taxpayer has some nonzero probability of being audited in a given year." See Kent W. Smith and Karyl A. Kinsey, "Cooperation and Control: Strategies and Tactics of Tax Administration," *Tax Administration Review,* forthcoming.

Selected AEI Publications

U.S. Fiscal Policy—Its Effects at Home and Abroad, John H. Makin (1986, 54 pp., $5.95)

Stockpiling Strategic Materials: An Evaluation of the National Program, Raymond F. Mikesell (1986, 68 pp., $5.95)

Essays in Contemporary Economic Problems: The Impact of the Reagan Program, Phillip Cagan, ed. (1986, 362 pp., cloth $20.95, paper $10.95)

The Politics of Industrial Policy, Claude E. Barfield and William A. Schambra, eds. (1986, 344 pp., cloth $20.95, paper $10.95)

Crisis in the Budget Process: Exercising Political Choice, Allen Schick, with papers by David Stockman, Rudolph Penner, Trent Lott, Leon Panetta, and Norman Ornstein (1986, 88 pp., $4.95)

Protectionism: Trade Policy in Democratic Societies, Jan Tumlir (1985, 72 pp., $4.95)

Real Tax Reform: Replacing the Income Tax, John H. Makin (1985, 42 pp., $3.95)

Entitlement Issues in the Domestic Budget: The Long-Term Agenda, John C. Weicher, ed. (1985, 52 pp., $4.95)

Essays in Contemporary Economic Problems: The Economy in Deficit, Phillip Cagan, ed. (1985, 336 pp., cloth $20.95, paper $9.95)

The R&D Tax Credit: Issues in Tax Policy and Industrial Innovation, Kenneth M. Brown, ed. (1984, 47 pp., $4.95)

Oil Price Shocks, Market Response, and Contingency Planning, George Horwich and David Leo Weimer (1984, 220 pp., cloth $16.95, paper $8.95)

Exchange Rates, Trade, and the U.S. Economy, Sven W. Arndt, Richard J. Sweeney, and Thomas D. Willett, eds. (1985, 296 pp., cloth $39.95)

Taxing the Family, Rudolph G. Penner, ed. (1983, 174 pp., cloth $15.95, paper $7.95)

Reforming the Income Tax System, William E. Simon (1981, 53 pp., $4.25)

• *Mail orders for publications to:* AMERICAN ENTERPRISE INSTITUTE, 4720 Boston Way, Lanham, MD 20706. • *For postage and handling, add 10 percent of total; minimum charge $2, maximum $10 (no charge on prepaid orders)* • *For information on orders, or to expedite service, call toll free 800-424-2873 (in Washington, D.C., 202-862-5869)* • *Prices subject to change without notice.* • *Payable in U.S. currency through U.S. banks only*